CONTENTS

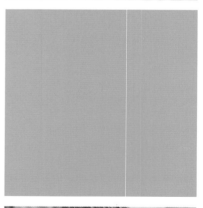

Time for School

To all the
teachers who
believed in me and,
more importantly,
taught me to believe
in myself.

PENGUIN BOOKS

UK | USA | Canada | Ireland | Australia | India | New Zealand | South Africa

Penguin Books is part of the Penguin Random House group of companies
whose addresses can be found at global.penguinrandomhouse.com.

Penguin
Random House
UK

First published 2021
001

Text and additional photography copyright © Daisy Upton, 2021
Photography copyright © Lol Johnson, 2021
Page 66 photography copyright © Cristina Pedreira Pèrez, 2020
Design © Nikki Dupin at Studio Nic&Lou
The moral right of the author and photographers has been asserted

The slime and play dough recipes for 'Messy Recipe Cards' are reproduced with kind permission of
Myriam Sandler (Instagram: @mothercould). Website home.oxfordowl.co.uk © Oxford University Press. *Highland
Games* (pictured on page 114) text copyright © Roderick Hunt; illustration copyright © Alex Brychta.
Questions from *Letters and Sounds: Principles and Practice of High Quality Phonics*, used in 'Yes/No Escape Room'
© Crown copyright, 2007. LEGO ® and LEGO DUPLO ® are trade marks of the LEGO group of companies.
Nintendo™, Nintendo Mario Bros and Mario Kart are trade marks of Nintendo. Every effort has been made to trace
copyright holders and to obtain their permission. The publisher apologizes for any errors or omissions and, if
notified of any corrections, will make suitable acknowledgement in future reprints or editions of this book.

This book includes references to third-party websites, which are controlled and maintained by others.
These links are included solely for the convenience of readers and do not constitute any endorsement by
Penguin Books Limited ('Penguin') of the sites linked or referred to, nor does Penguin have any control
over or responsibility for the content of any such sites.

Printed and bound in Italy

The authorized representative in the EEA is Penguin Random House Ireland,
Morrison Chambers, 32 Nassau Street, Dublin D02 YH68

A CIP catalogue record for this book is available from the British Library

ISBN: 978−0−241−50380−5

Five Minute Mum

Daisy Upton

Time for School

PENGUIN BOOKS

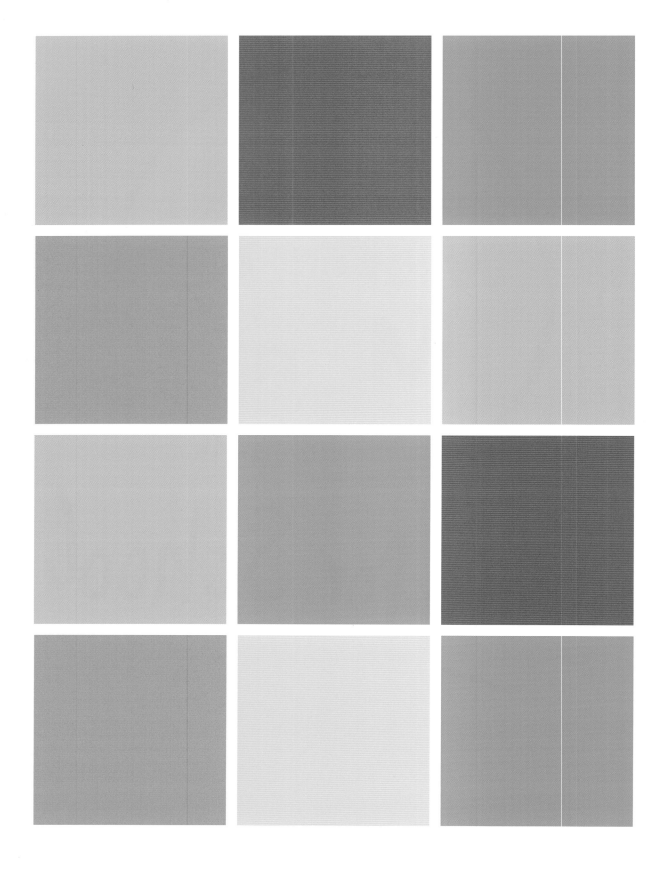

YOU ARE NOT A TEACHER

Let me begin by repeating this. **YOU ARE NOT A TEACHER**. Oh, unless you actually **ARE** a teacher, then hello! **MOST** of you are probably not qualified teachers. But I expect you are still a person who is in charge of young children for large portions of your day.

This book is not here to turn you into a teacher or tell you how to be a teacher at home. Those fantastic folks who take our kids off our hands for six hours a day, and fill their little minds with all kinds of wonderful knowledge, train for years to do that stuff. And they do it brilliantly. Having kids at home is a different thing entirely, and funnily enough it's the teachers who also happen to be parents that are often the first to agree with that!

So we've established that most of us don't have certificates to formally educate the small humans in our care. However, sometimes we do still need to teach our children stuff at home, don't we? But first I want to help unload some of the guilt you might be feeling right now. That niggling inner voice that sometimes whispers, 'You're not doing enough,' needs to be told to shut up. I am **FIVE MINUTE MUM**. And the reason I am writing this book is to invite you to become a **FIVE MINUTE PERSON** too. Whatever you are – mum, dad, grandparent, aunt, foster carer, whatever – join me in my five-minute mission. Little and often is the mantra, and guilt is given short shrift.

So what are we doing that takes five minutes then? My first book, *Give Me Five*, was filled with the games I played with my children when they were preschoolers – the games took five minutes to set up and gave them at least five minutes of fun. But, as quickly as I could write down all the ideas on to pages, our play evolved to fit around the school day – and, instead of keeping a toddler busy to buy me five minutes' peace, I found myself using my time to find ways to tie together homework and pleasure. An impossible task you might think!

I am very much hoping that this book will act like a little bridge: a paperbound stepping stone between what happens in the classroom and what happens at home. I wrote it to help people who are preparing their children to start school and also to offer guidance through their first few years of education, so you can learn together as you go. It's aimed at little ones aged between four and eight, but the games in the pages ahead can be easily adapted for kids of any age. I'm yet to meet a child (or person, for that matter) who doesn't prefer to learn through play.

Now, I don't know about you, but when my eldest started school I spent the first few months going 'Whaaaat?!' **AND** I had previously worked as a teaching assistant in reception class (that's the entry point to school in England, where I live)! Yet, still, most days I was baffled by the sheer volume of information I needed to keep in my head. I appeared to have taken on a secretarial job that I'd never interviewed for. I didn't feel qualified to remember harvest festival assembly dates and regular milk money payments, and then my eldest started to bring home BOOKS! Christ alive, I thought school meant I was going to have to do LESS: not frantically dig through the sofa cushions, yelling, 'Where is it? It's book change day and *Digby Dog Goes to London* is still missing! I don't want a letter from the teacher again!' as we simultaneously attempt to rush out of the door.

Oh, and the pressure! Those days that you DO forget the dinner money, or the 'wear your superhero pyjamas and bring in your favourite teacup' day, or whatever the heck it is, totally slips your addled mind . . . The eyes your child will give you as they relay the story (resulting from your forgetfulness) on your wet walk home will haunt you forever. The pressure comes not just from what you think the other seemingly organized parents might think but now it comes from your own disappointed offspring, too. Yikes.

And here's the other thing. You're sending them off to be educated and, wow, it's lovely, isn't it? What a weight lifted from the toddler years. Someone else is now teaching them every day and it's not costing you your life savings any more. Hurrah! But just as you've finished imagining what you're going to spend all the money on now you don't have what is essentially a second mortgage payment for your kid to go and paint somewhere else (just kidding, nurseries are flipping awesome!) then you hear the word '**HOMEWORK**' uttered. Oh god.

There is a proportion of your child's education that is down to you. Schools ease you in gently at first with reading books (in the beginning they don't even have any words – wahey! Easy this, innit?!) and a few simple words to learn. Then it's phonics. (Erm, OK, not quite sure on that, but surely I can google it . . . ?) Then, oh, there are also tricky words and high frequency words, and number bonds and spellings and times tables and ARRGGHHH!!!

It's actually quite a lot, isn't it? And here's the catch. It's not taught like it used to be! Oh no, sir, they don't teach Letterland in school like they did in the 80s and 90s, and sums aren't even called sums any more. It appears we now need an education to prepare for our child's education! Well, I hope that, instead of us going back to school ourselves, this book of games will do just the job!

The idea is that *Time for School* will be a handy helpful guide through the first three or so years of school – what here in England we call **RECEPTION**, **YEAR ONE** and **YEAR TWO**, or **EARLY YEARS FOUNDATION STAGE (EYFS)** and **KEY STAGE ONE**. Other countries call them Grades or Ps (as in the Scottish P1, P2, etc.) or any number of things (really, guys, can we all not just agree on one way?!) . . .

I truly hope that this book will be able to explain it all in my usual simple five-minute style to help you understand what is really expected from your little ones. How you can help them at home without tearing your hair out or wanting to bang your head against the kitchen table. How you can spend five minutes here and there supporting them with fun and games together so it isn't just homework – it's quality family time. This book has been designed to be dipped in and out of, depending on what level your child is at, what homework has been sent home, or what concerns you might have about the education system or how schools work. You don't need to read it all in one go. After all, we are busy people, aren't we? No one's got time for it all. I sure as hell know I don't. I get my exercise in nowadays after shouting, 'Oh balls!' when I've checked the clock at 2:55 p.m. and have to leg it to the school gates, arriving red-faced and puffing.

So, no, you are **NOT** a teacher* and neither do you need to be to support your children through these early school years.

You need to care for and nurture your little ones. Foster and encourage a love of learning and discovery. Develop curiosity. Provide a listening ear and be their cheerleader. And then all the usual other stuff like, you know, feeding them and keeping them from jumping off the top of the sofa. That, too! But let the teachers teach and, instead, let us as parents, carers and guardians spend those precious one-to-one minutes with our kids at home playing, laughing, being silly and having fun. Because it is in those moments, really, that they are learning what the secret to true happiness is – finding the joy in the everyday. Five minutes at a time.

* Even if you are a qualified teacher, I bet you often find it easier having a class of thirty than one or two of your own little nose-miners!!! There's no PGCE for parenting, is there?! So I hope this book might still come in handy, and – if nothing else – perhaps be a reference for you to direct parents to.

DOES THE GOLDEN RULE STILL APPLY?

Ah, my GOLDEN RULE. This is the rule I have always applied to every activity and game I play with my kids and it is this:

LET THE CHILD COME TO THE GAME.

Set up the game first, in a place they can't see or when they aren't around if at all possible, and then let them discover it and decide if and when they want to play. This way they take control and, more often than not, are intrigued enough to want to join in with the game. And all of a sudden you're learning through play together without them even realizing. I started following this rule when my kids were toddlers and it revolutionized our playtime.

But does this still apply as our kids get older? When they were tiny, it encouraged them to learn through play in a way that took the pressure off us all. If they didn't want to do it, we didn't. And that was that. Life made easy. In five minutes I could put it away again and no damage was done.

Now, when it comes to homework that has a deadline, it isn't quite the same, is it? So my advice, when it comes to children aged four and up, is to continue to try wherever you can to implement the GOLDEN RULE but know that it won't always be possible. If you're practising spellings (page 156) or times tables (page 226) and want to play those particular games regularly then just set them up and see what happens. If you have early risers like I do, I often find that first thing in the morning is best. Or I set them up ready for when we come home after school. As we clatter through the door laden with bags, I know that 'Is there a game, Mum?' will be the next question out of their mouths, because this is just part of our routine. If there isn't one, they are disappointed! (I know – what have I done?!!)

But sometimes there is no child-led option. Things need to be done, and in some schools there might be consequences for not doing it. In these situations I often resort to reward systems to encourage my two if they are feeling particularly reluctant. I use their passions, whatever they may be, and say for every ten minutes they do their homework they get those minutes back to do something they enjoy – playing a board game with me, playing computer games or playing out with friends. For all of us, often the thought of a treat at the end of something resembling a chore can be a huge motivator. It will, of course, be trial and error, and whatever works for you as a family is always best.

Another part of my GOLDEN RULE is that you do the activity with them or start the game first to see if this encourages them to join in. I've found that this is still valid and helpful as they get older. As their reliance on us lessens, we end up spending a bit less time with them, so play can be a way of grabbing one of those rare one-to-one moments together. Often kids are much more willing to seize that opportunity than we might imagine. If your child enjoys screen time and you're keen to get them away from it, setting up a game in their eye-line is a great way to distract them. Ewan was once playing on his iPad and I laid out a game right in front of him and started playing it with Flo. He soon tossed Minecraft aside and started hopping around the lounge with us. Resistance was futile. FOMO is strong in kiddos, especially when they hear laughter.

These days, although I have found the GOLDEN RULE isn't essential any more to encourage Ewan and Florence to play a game where we are also learning, it's still very helpful. Our routine of one or two five-minute games a day works well, and I have found that, once they're in the swing of it, there's no encouragement required. Kids love to play, especially with the people they love most – that's just how it is.

So my GOLDEN RULE has been amended to this:

JUST KEEP TRYING.

It goes without saying that it's best if there's an adult to watch kiddos as they play, especially if they're using safety scissors, throwing stuff or jumping around!

Look out for the colours of the side headings! They're there to help you quickly find the section you need as you flick through the book.

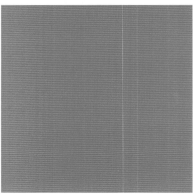

USING THIS BOOK

Before you delve into this book, I want to note a few things here that you may find helpful to have or to know. The sole purpose of these bound-together pages is to make the curriculum and your child's learning less confusing, so here are my five top tips for using this book and getting the most out of the games with as little effort as possible. After all, I promised you five-minute set-ups, didn't I?

1. MAKE YOUR OWN FLASH CARDS

You can buy brilliant flash cards, of course, and I have a few sets myself, but mostly I prefer to make my own because, as the weeks and terms whizz by, my children are learning new things all the time. Often words, phonics sounds or times tables will be sent home on worksheets to learn, and flash cards are pretty much the same thing: bits of paper with things to learn on them. So with these few items I can make flash cards at home in minutes:

- coloured card and/or paper and/or craft foam
- a marker pen
- scissors
- elastic bands or sandwich bags or envelopes

Now, whenever something is sent home to learn, I immediately knock up a set of flash cards. (I usually make two sets of the same cards as often my games involve matching things up.) Then I put an elastic band round them or pop them in an envelope and leave them somewhere in the kitchen within easy reach, so that whenever the need should arise, they are there to grab, and off we go.

Ideally use black pen on coloured card or paper, and write clearly. You can use both upper-case and lower-case letters, as children need to know both, but favour lower-case letters because this is what we mostly see when we read. For anything that usually has a capital letter, such as their name, include it.

SOME USEFUL THINGS TO HAVE ON FLASH CARDS INCLUDE:

- **Phonics sounds and words** (Phase 2 pages 68–71; Phase 3 pages 84–87; Phase 4 pages 96–97; Phase 5 pages 106–111; Phase 6 pages 118–119)
- **High frequency words** (pages 124–125)
- **Number bonds** (pages 204–205)
- **Times tables** (pages 228–229)

When making up cards with numbers, I tend to write the number sentences (sums to you and me!) on one bit of card and the answers on another, as games often require them to be matched up.

It's also useful to have numbers 0 to 20 on their own, as well as the symbols + − x ÷ = in addition to a general alphabet set with each letter on one card.

2. MAKE YOUR OWN NUMBER LINE

This is a useful resource to keep handy. A number line can act as a visual aid for children counting forward and backwards, or for adding and taking away. It can also help them to see numbers in chunks for times tables.

The image below is an example of what I mean by a number line. Use a piece of cardboard to create one of your own to have on hand for any number-based games or homework. You can also create number grids for times tables as shown on pages 228–229.

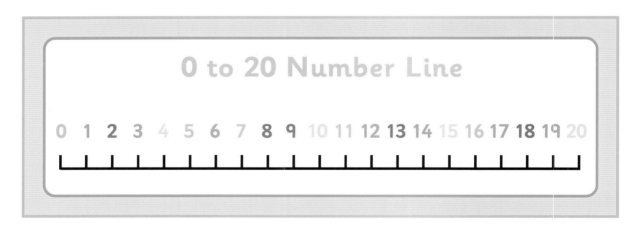

0 to 20 Number Line

0 1 2 3 4 5 6 7 8 9 10 11 12 13 14 15 16 17 18 19 20

3. THE TAT BOX

Another handy bit of kit for the games in this book is my trusty tat box. It's a box full of all the plastic bits and pieces that my kids get from magazines, parties, fast-food meals and so on. (Shoeboxes are perfect for this!) I store it out of reach, so that when needed I can pull it out, and the kids go nuts over it. It frequently buys me some rainy-day peace, but I also found it incredibly helpful to support learning as small toys can instantly jazz up an otherwise dull activity.

4. TERMINOLOGY

Because the purpose of this book is to try to decode what is happening in the classroom for us adults at home, I have sometimes shied away from terms that would be used in schools and instead favoured more straightforward ways of explaining things. I try to write as if I'm chatting to a friend over a coffee rather than as a teacher discussing it with a fellow professional. So there may be things in here that as an educational professional you wouldn't perhaps say in the classroom, but I have used them to help break down the complexities of our schooling system. However, I have included formal glossaries to cover terminology where I think it's helpful on pages 41–42 for **PHONICS** and 193 for **MATHS**.

5. MIX IT UP

Lots of the games in this book can be played in multiple ways. For example, a game like Wrecking Ball on page 59 features in the Phonics Phase 2 section, but it's really just a **RECOGNITION** game, which means it is purely about your child reading, or recognizing the thing you are playing with. This means it can be played with anything that your child needs to learn to recognize, including sounds in any phase of phonics, high frequency words or spellings, or numbers.

The games that can be adapted have this **RECOGNITION GAME** star on the page. This is to remind you that you can interchange the words, sounds or numbers with anything that your child is focusing on at the moment.

Please do vary and mix them up in any way you like to suit whatever it is your child is trying to practise at home. The best way to learn something new is through repeated exposure in different ways, so use the resources in this book to bring some fun and laughter into learning.

THE BUILDING BLOCKS OF LEARNING

We all learn things differently. Our brains are so amazingly complex that when it comes to storing information and retrieving it in times of need, every single one of us does it in our own way.

I don't know about you, but sometimes mine doesn't seem to work at all. I will stare at an object and wonder what on earth it's called, as the cogs in my head whirl continuously and my mind comes up blank. Or someone will approach me and say 'Hello!' in a familiar way and, as I smile back nervously, my brain is screaming,

'WHERE DO YOU KNOW HER FROM? IS IT SWIMMING TOTS? PILATES? AN OLD ENEMY FROM SCHOOL???'

Yes, brains are mysterious. And, when it comes to children and the way their brains learn, it's patience that we need buckets of. Now I know this isn't always easy. When you and your child have read the word 'look' eight times in a book already and on the ninth time they still stare blankly at the word on the page, you do want to lob said book out of the nearest window (I know – I've been there too!). But I have a theory that helps me out, and I'll explain it to you here in case it is useful for you, too.

I like to see learning as a big load of **BUILDING BLOCKS**. You know, the kind of blocks you play with when children are little: lots of colours and shapes and sizes used to build teetering towers for chubby little fists to knock over.

So, for each thing we need to learn, there is a height or level we are trying to get to. Take the example I just mentioned – learning to read the word 'look'. The level we're trying to reach is the child seeing the word 'look' and immediately being able to read it and say 'look'. That's our goal; the goal is at a certain height and we need blocks to get there.

In order to get to that goal, we need to provide learning opportunities that teach your kiddo to read the word 'look'. Each one of these opportunities is a block for our tower. So, when we read to them at night and point at the word 'look' on the page as we read it aloud, that's one block. It goes on the stack.

Your child might then do a phonics session at school that teaches them that when we see 'o' and 'o' together, we read that as the 'oo' sound, which we hear in the word 'look'. That's another block added on.

Now, some of the blocks are tiny. A block can be us saying the word 'look' in passing. Or your child learning the sound the letter 'l' makes. But they are all tiny moments of learning, building us up to the goal level.

Some children might only need three blocks to learn the word 'look'. Their brains might just work in such a way with letters that, once they have seen it a couple of times, they have got it stored in their memory. Their blocks to get to that goal level were big and chunky and all the same colour, shape and size. They were shown the word 'look' on a bit of paper a few times and one, two, three, boom! They got it!

For other children, their blocks might be different. They might need loads of tiny blocks of learning to get to the same level. They might need to see the 'oo' twenty different ways for it to stick in their head. They might require varied sensory input like writing 'look' in sand, or walking around giant Os in chalk, or reading it in five different books. Their learning blocks are smaller, and are many shapes and colours. But they are still building each time, stacking each block to get to that goal in their own time.

Some children who might take over a hundred blocks to get the hang of number bonds to 10 (pages 204–205) might only need a couple of blocks to learn all the sounds for Phase 3 in phonics (pages 84–85). We are all different. But each bit of learning is a block, a step up, and is added to the tower to reach that end goal, whatever it may be.

I guess what I'm trying to say here is this: **KEEP AT IT**. It might feel at times like you are getting nowhere as your little one is unknowingly stacking these blocks of learning. You might feel you've played some of these games ten times and your kiddo hasn't moved forward, but they *have* – it's just invisible. Every time you do any tiny thing, it's a block in place, and it is building something worthwhile and important. One day they will hit that goal level and you'll see it. There's no feeling quite like it. And, of course, there are always more stacks to build. Even for us grown-ups. We are still building with our own blocks. So keep on stacking. It all counts.

THE SCHOOL–HOME RELATIONSHIP

I have heard it said (many a time in staffrooms across the various schools I've worked in) that when asked 'What's the most difficult thing about being a teacher?' a teacher will often jokingly reply: 'The parents!'

As a parent, **I GET IT**. We carefully nurture these precious little things we created and then all of a sudden we have to hand them over to another adult we don't even know for a big chunk of the day. We're left out on the playground to gather tiny reluctant snippets of info from our kids while the teacher is privy to all that's going on. The teachers know their levels, what's expected of them, the embarrassing facts that kids love to share ('My mummy has a hairy tuppence' was the best one I was ever told in the classroom!). As a parent, it's quite hard. How much would you love to be a fly on the wall just for a day?!

I think the thing that is most difficult is that there needs to be an element of trust, but we don't get masses of time to build that. We just have to have it. Between teachers and the adults responsible for each child, there are multiple forms of communication. Parents' evenings, notes sent home in schoolbags, reading record scribbles, 'Can I have a quick word?' chats on the playground, as well as emails. Some of these can get lost in translation or be misunderstood, and I have at times seen frustration build on both sides. Playground chatter between parents can swing between hugely helpful to massively confusing, depending on how and when the information is passed over.

When I worked with children with additional learning challenges, I sometimes found their parents had grown up with similar challenges, or their own fear of school and education was clearly apparent. It reminded me that everyone comes with their own story, and the best way to build trust is to move forward with patience and understanding, while ensuring that the child is always put first.

Which is why, if there is something big happening at home or in your child's life, it is really useful for the teacher to know this. If someone who usually lives in the child's house has moved out or they've experienced the death of someone close, or anything at all that might affect their world, then please pass that information on to the school if you feel you can. If a teacher knows a child is going through something particularly difficult outside school, they can help to support in many different ways.

When it comes to **COMMUNICATING**, there are definitely challenges on both sides. As a teacher, you are trying to carefully get across as much information as is needed without bombarding parents with stuff that isn't necessary for them to know. It's a fine balance, as some parents wish they knew more, and others are begging to be told less. Teachers are often trying to encourage parents to become involved with their child's learning, knowing their support is vital to a child's success in education, but are also aware that too much pressure won't help anyone.

So, if at any point as a parent, you are finding it all hugely confusing, then please **REACH OUT** to the teachers. Ask to talk to them or write them a note. Perhaps, before you go, make a list of all the things you want to talk to them about. It's totally natural that some people feel intimidated in a school setting, so to save yourself any anxiety, scribble down your thoughts and questions first to make sure you cover everything you wish to know.

During my time as a teaching assistant I supported many different teachers in the classroom and, despite their differing styles and personalities, I know we all had one thing in common: we were fiercely protective of all the children in that class and wanted to get the absolute **BEST** out of every single one of them. As a parent, it's nice to remind ourselves of this and, as cheesy as it sounds, try to see ourselves and our children's teacher as a team working towards the same goal.

If you are having any issues, please remember that every school has a list of policies which should be available on their website or ask the headteacher to see them. These will give you details on how the school should handle everything from complaints of bullying to their disciplinary procedures, school rules and classroom management.

COMPARISON

You might have heard this before. It's a phrase attributed to the late US President Theodore Roosevelt, but it's more apt now than ever in this age of social media and it's this:

'COMPARISON IS THE THIEF OF JOY.'

It truly is. If we compare ourselves or our children to other people, we are often taking away a bit of our joy. Florence learned to ride her bike relatively early – certainly much earlier than Ewan did. She did this because, during the first national lockdown of the 2020 pandemic, there wasn't a lot else to do except ride bikes and scooters around our cul-de-sac. She watched Ewan doing it every day, and was motivated to want to join him, so she took it upon herself to learn. And learn she did.

Now if I were to compare Ewan to her, who learned when he was probably a whole year older than Flo, I might feel disappointed. He took much longer. He didn't get it as quickly and wasn't as self-motivated. All that comparison does is dim the immense pleasure we all gained from watching Ewan learn to ride his bike.

I think the trap we can sometimes fall into as parents is to think, for some reason, that faster is better, or sooner is better. When in reality it isn't, is it? Do you go into a job interview now and boast that you were weaned at five months, or that you walked at twelve months? Of course not. Yet we are constantly comparing our babies to our friends' children to see who is hitting what milestones and when.

Comparison is a natural response in us all as humans. And it can be massively helpful. By assessing and comparing our children, educators can identify children who require additional support or who might have special educational needs that haven't been diagnosed or spotted yet. It is comparison that gives us developmental stages and baseline measures.

But don't forget that within these stages and measures there are huge scopes of what is considered neurotypical. And just because one child learns to use scissors a full year after another child doesn't determine their path in life.

So, don't let your joy be stolen. Celebrate every small win your child makes. Let them take their own path and go at their own rate. This goes for you, too! Stop comparing yourself to other adults standing on that playground. To the child running out of those school doors, you are the person they want to see. To them you are perfect, and that is really what matters.

SPECIAL EDUCATIONAL NEEDS & DISABILITIES (SEND)

My first job as a teaching assistant was to provide one-to-one support to a little boy (who we'll call Liam) in a preschool class. He had what was classed as special educational needs (though I'm aware many people hate this phrase) relating to his behaviour and speech. To help me, the school arranged for me to do specialist training to support children with speech and language difficulties and challenging behaviour. It was an invaluable insight into the fact that not all children gain the most from standard educational practices, and that the challenges that these children and their families face are varied and unique.

Over the course of that year, I sat in on meetings with various people from the local authority and supported the parents through the statement process (which was, at the time, how a child was assessed to decide what additional support they qualified for). I worked with speech and language therapists, welfare managers and the school's **SENCO**. I got to see both points of view – the frustration of the parents who just wanted the best for their son, and the constraints on the school with regard to budget, staff and classroom management.

There was a lot of paperwork, as well as meetings, but ultimately what it came down to was this child. A little boy who saw the world differently. He couldn't speak aloud his frustrations and he sometimes missed out on experiences that other children his age were gaining. His needs in some respects might well have been 'special' but what he taught me during our year together was that nearly all his needs were exactly the same as mine. To be loved, to learn, to have friends, to be listened to and to be happy.

I will never ever forget the first time he said my name or the gratitude his parents showed me. Recently his dad messaged me through my social media channels to say he remembered me! I could not have been more thrilled to hear how well his (now much bigger) boy was doing.

So, if you have a child at school who has special educational needs or you have had a conversation with a teacher about how they think additional support might be required for your child, I am afraid I can't tell you anything about how things might unfold. The reason for this is because the main thing I learned is that every child and circumstance is unique. Even if your child has a diagnosis for something that has a specific term (like autism), each child responds differently to the school environment and the people they will meet, which I'm sure, as a parent, you already know. I know that for many, with funding and budget cuts, it is a constant battle to get the level of support needed. I know that it can be incredibly frustrating taking on a complicated system to get the right support for your child, but I also do know that the teachers, teaching assistants and SENCOs are on your side and are there to help you through it. They too want what is best for your child and will try to do whatever is in their power to assist the process.

The thing I found most helpful was keeping the lines of communication open and regular. As a teaching assistant I spoke to the parents as often as I could. The SENCO relayed information to me that was useful. The speech therapist was updated on Liam's progress and setbacks regularly. Those with experience of the process helped with advice or recommendations. My advice would be to seek the support of other parents if you can, through online support groups or charities. Their advice is invariably the best and most up-to-date and there is great comfort to be found in a shared experience.

During my time as a teaching assistant, I discovered that visual timetables and picture representations of emotions were the most useful tools when working with children who required additional support. I used to make them myself by taking pictures of things familiar to them to prompt what we were doing next, or images of our faces to discuss feelings if they were struggling to find the words.

I often get asked for game recommendations for children with a specific disability or learning challenge, but my response is no different to what I'd say to someone asking on behalf of a neurotypical or physically able child: 'What are they interested in?' This is the key to unlocking everything. Once I found what made Liam laugh, everything became much simpler. The games always revolved around that. Many of the games in this book can be adapted. Use whatever your child is most interested in or gains the most joy from and weave that into the play, and the learning will follow.

Every school will have a SENCO - Special Educational Need Co-Ordinator - who is specifically trained and assigned to support children with SEND.

In England, there are currently two levels of additional support in education: SEN support and an EHC (Education, Health and Care) plan. For more information, visit www.gov.uk/children-with-special-educational-needs

Some helpful organizations that provide support networks include:
- family-action.org.uk
- contact.org.uk
- councilfordisabled children.org.uk

DYSLEXIA

If we haven't directly experienced dyslexia ourselves, either by being diagnosed with it or knowing someone who has, we can often reduce it to believing it's something to do with reversing Bs and Ds when writing.

Now, while this can be a sign of it, dyslexia is a lot more complex. Let me start by saying I am by no means an expert in dyslexia. When I first decided to become a qualified teaching assistant, I completed a Level 5 CPD Award in Supporting Adults with Dyslexia and Co-occurring Difficulties through the charity Dyslexia Action, because I felt it would be helpful to me. And invariably it was.

Dyslexia, according to the NHS website (www.nhs.uk/conditions/dyslexia), is:

> 'A common learning difficulty that can cause problems with reading, writing and spelling. It's a specific learning difficulty, which means it causes problems with certain abilities used for learning, such as reading and writing. Unlike a learning disability, intelligence isn't affected.
>
> It's estimated up to 1 in every 10 people in the UK has some degree of dyslexia. Dyslexia is a lifelong problem that can present challenges on a daily basis, but support is available to improve reading and writing skills and help those with the problem be successful at school and work.'

So why am I talking about this here? Well, I think when children are learning how to read and write they can sometimes do things like reverse their Bs and Ds or write backwards, or repeatedly get stuck on particular words – all of which might make parents worry that their child has dyslexia and they aren't being supported correctly. For a few children this will be the case. However, for the majority, this is simply part of their learning and development. All those things – including letter reversal, mirror writing and backwards writing – are incredibly common in children learning to write.

Because of this, children aren't usually assessed for dyslexia until they are around the age of seven or above. This allows time for children to move fully through the developmental phases before judgements on their learning are made. However, if you have any concerns at all about your child at any age when it comes to dyslexia or co-occurring difficulties, then please speak to the **SENCO** (see page 17) at your school. They will be able to advise and support you and your child with any difficulties they might be having with their reading and writing.

PARENTS WITH DYSLEXIA

Sometimes I receive messages from parents who have dyslexia themselves and are anxious about supporting their children with their learning at home. I believe that when it comes to helping people with dyslexia learn best, those that have it can be a great asset to their children. I'm a huge advocate of learning in many different ways and especially through multi-sensory play. If you, as a dyslexic person, teach your child exactly the way you would like to be taught things, then you can't go wrong. Whether it's through playing games with them or physically moving your body to get to know the letters and sounds, or using different techniques of your own that you've developed over the years, giving your child access to lots of different approaches to learning can only be a good thing.

It's also hugely confidence-boosting for children if they can correct us as grown-ups. If we do make a mistake, then our kids are the first to call us on it. It's always best to give them praise for spotting it, reminding them that it happens to everyone, and let them take pride in their knowledge. My mum was never formally diagnosed with dyslexia, but I sincerely believe she has it. She supported me to read and write throughout my childhood, and I went to university to do a degree in English and sport science. She reads a novel a week and I grew up watching her read for pleasure, which encouraged me to do the same. So please don't ever feel that, because you are a parent with dyslexia, you aren't able to support your children's learning. You can and you will.

THINGS YOU CAN DO TO SUPPORT CHILDREN WHO ARE FINDING READING AND WRITING PARTICULARLY TRICKY:

- **Hold a ruler** (on its blank reverse side) under words in reading books, so they can follow the text along a line.

- **Place transparent coloured overlays over white pages of text** – black text on a coloured background can help people with dyslexia to read, like we've done on these two pages. If you can't print on to coloured paper, then an overlay can help.

- **Keep playing** – introduce letters in lots of fun ways. Do it little and often, and try to find the format that best suits your child, which will mean they will be better able to remember the letters and words.

- **Use as much imagery as you can.** Draw pictures around letters and sounds. Talk about the shapes of the letters or things they remind you of. Sound Art on page 77 is a great game to use for this.

- For more information and support please visit the British Dyslexia Association's website: www.bdadyslexia.org.uk

HOMEWORK

What I am talking about here is activities or tasks set for children to do at home, **IN ADDITION** to reading and learning their spellings and times tables. Sometimes they are one and the same thing. But, when it comes to tasks like a worksheet that asks your child to 'Write five sentences about your bedroom', I am of the opinion that I don't like it. Never mind what my kids think, I HATE IT!

So there, I've said it. I am totally on board with reading, and spellings and times tables. For kids aged between four and eight I think that is plenty to do already. I've read different studies that look at children around the world and the effects of homework on their learning. The results differ: some suggest it's massively beneficial; others suggest it isn't and actually widens the gap of learning for children from more disadvantaged backgrounds.

Let me say, though, that I completely understand why teachers give homework. It's an attempt to get parents involved with their child's learning and also for the child to take on a bit of independence and responsibility for their own schoolwork in a different environment.

However, I also believe that if the style of the homework is as dull as a worksheet, it takes away from one of the most important elements of their development: **PLAY**. Kids at this age still have a strong desire and urge to play, and I'm not particularly keen on anything that takes that playtime away. I also think the pressure on parents to take homework on as an additional responsibility is immense. If you have reading, spellings and times tables to work on and THEN you also get a worksheet sent home that says your child must write out five sentences about their bedroom, it's too much. And don't forget that I am a Stay at Home Parent. I have time after school to do this. Most parents I know work and don't have the hours of 4–6 p.m. on a weekday to do activities. For many of my friends, helping their kiddos with homework ends up eating into their family time at a weekend, which I think is a bit rubbish really.

Now you can completely and utterly disagree with me. I understand that many will and that is totally fine. But all I am saying here is that if you also find it just a bit much, and have a child you have to battle with to get homework done, I hear you. It isn't easy. So here are a few things that might be useful to try:

1. **CHANGE IT UP.** Turn the task they've been given into a treasure hunt around the house, or list it out in masking tape, or write it on the windows with a dry-wipe pen. Use bottle tops with numbers written on them for maths tasks or home-made flash cards for letters. See if there is any way you can make it more exciting, more physical, and mix it up if at all possible.

2. **MAKE HOMEWORK PART OF YOUR ROUTINE.** Do little and often and make it a daily thing. So, even if they don't have homework that day, call it 'daily challenge time' and use it to do something together. Read, play a five-minute game or get some fun activity books and do one page with them. Make it short and simple, so when they do get homework you could always do it over the course of a few days, a few minutes at a time. It's just part of that regular challenge time.

3. **USE TECHNOLOGY THEY ENJOY.** For older ones, tell them to go and do their homework in their bedroom and you will video-call them from downstairs to help or they have to email or text you questions and answers. Even using a keyboard is sometimes enough to encourage them to want to have a go at writing or finding out information.

4. **TURN IT INTO A COMPETITION.** Join in with them and have a go too. Perhaps mark each other's work at the end with ticks, or write a comment saying what you like the most about it. Use a timer and see if you can both beat the clock. Obviously you might want to slow down to their level, but just having you sitting there and doing it too can be enough to make them want to do it.

5. **USE THEIR FAVOURITE TOY.** If the homework is to learn phonics sounds, and their favourite toy is a train – put the sounds around the track and tell them they need to collect from all the 'stations' – each sound is a station at which they need to tell you where the train is going next. If they love puzzles, write words out on a bit of paper and cut it up randomly to make a puzzle. Use whatever they love to inspire and motivate them.

If homework is becoming an issue at home, talk to the teacher. Explain what the sticking points are for you or your child, as they will often be able to support with advice and suggestions.

HOW TO GET KIDS TO TELL YOU ABOUT THEIR DAY

ME: 'Have you had a good day?'

MY KID: 'Yeah.'

ME: 'What did you do?'

MY KID: 'I can't remember.'

ME: 'You must remember something?'

MY KID: 'Erm. No.'

ME: 'OK.' *remains baffled as to what my child has done for six hours of the day*

Sound familiar?

It used to drive me mad when I was a teaching assistant. I would have carefully carried out a whole day of fun activities playing with letters in sand, creating a treasure hunt of numbers around the playground, Tuff Tray set-ups with games and puzzles, songs, jokes and laughter – and I would hear a kid telling their parent they had done 'nothing much'!

I used to want to shout over the fence: 'Errr, excuse me, but actually that's utter rubbish! Let me give you a rundown!' I couldn't believe the little blighters didn't tell their parents a single thing we had done!

THEN I HAD KIDS OF MY OWN.

And I got the exact same response and I KNEW they were talking baloney. So how to get it out of them? Well, here are my five tips for chatting about the day with your children:

1. **ASK SOMETHING SPECIFIC BUT THE SAME THING EVERY DAY.** So, for example, you might say, 'What did you have for your pudding today?' And they might at first reply that they don't know or shrug. But, if you keep asking that same question every day, then hopefully one of the days when they are getting their pudding from the midday assistants it might pop into their head that they are asked about this at home, so maybe they will tell you later. This happened with Ewan on his first few days. He told me about having a jacket potato, and so every day I would ask, 'Did

you have a jacket potato?' And he would then launch into a story about how he had or hadn't. He knew what question was coming, so he had stored that in his memory to tell me.

2. **TRY TO RESIST THE URGE TO BOMBARD THEM WITH THINGS LIKE:** 'Did you have a good day?' 'What did you do?' 'Who did you play with?' Just like us, sometimes our little ones need to decompress after a busy day and having questions fired at them won't help at all. So maybe just stay a bit quiet for a while and see if they then initiate the conversation.

3. **IF AT ALL POSSIBLE, HAVE A SHORT WALK.** Either park the car a bit further away or walk home if you can. This gives you time together, and walking also seems to work really nicely to facilitate chatting. There's probably a very scientific reason behind it, but I know that me and my two have had some of our most enlightening chats when we stroll the twenty minutes home from school.

4. **IF THEY DON'T WANT TO CHAT AT ALL, TELL THEM ABOUT YOUR DAY.** Explain what you've had for lunch and where you've been. Then they can see the conversation modelled when you ask, 'What did you do today?' They understand exactly what kind of details you are asking for and can mirror and mimic you. I often get interrupted when I tell them about my day as it suddenly triggers their memory.

5. **PLAY A GAME.** When you get in from school, play for five minutes. It's amazing what information they will suddenly drop into conversation when you're engaged in play, especially role play with dolls or figures. We also often finish with a hot chocolate, which is another great chat encourager.

When I shared these tips on social media, I received a lot of replies from folks telling me what they do. Here are some of the really wonderful ideas that came out:

- Some people said they ask their kids to share one good thing and one bad thing. They said their children's willingness to share tales about other children being told off often got the conversation going!

- Lots of people said bedtime was a great time to talk. It often meant their kids were cleverly delaying sleep time but they didn't mind as they got cosy in bed and had a good natter.

- Open-ended questions are always better. Try not to ask ones with a yes or no answer but instead say 'What was your favourite part of today?' Or 'What made you smile today?'

- Asking silly questions or opposite questions can also be good. 'I bet you didn't go outside today?' 'Wasn't Mrs Moo Moo your teacher today?'

SATS, ASSESSMENTS AND TESTS

At various points throughout their schooling, children are going to be assessed on how they are progressing with their learning. Teachers do this in a variety of ways. During the early years foundation stage (EYFS) little ones are assessed through play and observation. They will be encouraged to play certain games or complete little tasks in the classroom as part of their play and, as they do it, teachers will be watching them carefully and assessing their ability. This is all regularly recorded and shared with you in reports or at parents' evening. They will flag any concerns or areas they think your child needs to work on, or tell you if they think they require additional classroom support or outside agency support from people like psychologists or speech and language therapists and so on. Likewise, they will mention if your child is particularly gifted, as each school has their own programme and ways to encourage and support these children further.

As children move into Key Stage 1, the assessment becomes slightly more formal. Children will often have separate workbooks for different parts of their learning, and the teacher will mark and assess these weekly to track their progress. It's wonderful when you're invited into the school, or shown these workbooks at parents' evening, to see your child's work and how it develops as they progress through the year!

Although I know it won't be the same for everyone, here is a short guide to some of the assessments that you and your child can expect during these first years at school in England.

PHONICS SCREENING

Towards the end of Year One (ages five to six) teachers carry out a simple, brief assessment of each child in their class, looking at whether they can recognize phonics sounds in real and nonsense words made up of phonics sounds they've been taught. They just have to read them, and the teacher notes down how many they are able to read correctly. The results are recorded for the school and national standards.

Now this, and any other assessment, isn't anything to be worried about. It's only for the schools and teaching staff to understand how effective their phonics teaching system is and to identify any children who might need additional support with phonics and reading.

As I always tell parents and caregivers, children all develop differently. For many, this screening comes at a time when your kiddo is already confident with the sounds they've been learning. For others, they might not be quite there yet, but it's much better that teachers know where the gaps in their knowledge and understanding might be, in order to give them additional support. The only thing I would suggest you do at home to prepare your children for this assessment is **PLAY**! Phonics games can be found starting on page 53 of this book.

SATS (STANDARD ASSESSMENT TESTS / NATIONAL CURRICULUM TESTS)

In England at the end of Year Two (ages six to seven) children have SATs. These are a series of test papers for the children to complete. They aren't strictly timed and children are given lots of breaks between each paper, so they will just seem like part of a typical school day. The tests are the kind of activities they will be used to, like reading a paragraph of text and then answering some questions about it. The teachers will mark the papers and give the children a score, which will show how well your child has done against the expected national standard.

THE PAPERS THEY WILL COMPLETE ARE:

- two papers on READING
- two papers on MATHEMATICS
- two papers on English grammar, punctuation and SPELLING

My advice is that to prepare them for this you need to do what I am always going to suggest throughout this book: **PLAY!** The reason this book has a chapter each on reading, writing and spelling, and maths is because these are the core subjects, and the reason why each chapter has lots of ways to make that learning just one big load of games is because this is how kids learn best. So just keep playing.

If you, or your child, feels anxious about the assessment, please remind yourselves it is as much for the teachers and school as it is for your child. It is for the staff to understand how well their teaching methods are working and to put things in place to either continue as they are or to implement new strategies to improve. These scores will not determine the future success of your little one. It is simply a guide.

If you wish to know more, there is more support and a fantastic explanation of SATs on the Oxford Owl website: home.oxfordowl.co.uk

HOME-SCHOOLING

Now, obviously this book's title and everything in it refers to children who are attending mainstream school. But I understand, of course, that not everyone makes this choice for their family. I want to make a note here to say that if you are using this book to support your home-schooling I am very glad. I believe that every family should make decisions based on what is right for them. As we all now know, thanks to the lockdowns in 2020, home-schooling is by no means easy!

If you have taken this decision for you and your family, I massively admire you as, despite my years of experience as a teaching assistant, I honestly don't believe I could do it full-time.

So regardless of whether your kiddo is home-schooled or attends a formal school setting, this book is for anybody who is wanting to support their little ones with their learning. And if you are in two minds as to whether to home-school or send your child to a mainstream school either part- or full-time, then I hope this book provides some insight and clarity into both worlds to help inform the choice that is best for you.

ENGLISH AS AN ADDITIONAL LANGUAGE (EAL)

If you're raising your children to be bilingual, or English isn't your first language, supporting your child with their learning at home (especially when it comes to phonics), might seem even more confusing or intimidating. You might find some sounds really hard to model for your children, or worry about keeping a second language relevant for them when they start spending all day, every day, in a mostly English-speaking environment.

At first it could seem like bilingual children are behind in their language compared to their peers, but actually speech therapists would explain how they aren't at all, because when counting how many words a child can say or understand, the therapists include both languages. Children who learn two or more languages at the same time gradually catch up with their peers as they learn and play, so do what comes naturally to you. Speak to them in your native language, mix and match, and have as much fun with language as you can. To children, all language is new, so it's the perfect time to introduce more than one way of communicating. The educational, cultural and neurological benefits of being raised bilingual are **HUGE** and lifelong, so don't get discouraged if it feels a little tough at times. Talk to your child's teacher or other school leaders for guidance on how best to support them at home, and most of all be kind to yourself – learning another language is a real achievement and something I very much wish I had mastered!

There are some amazing resources online for parents raising their kids to be bilingual. This National Literacy Trust has particularly helpful information about a lot of different languages: literacytrust.org.uk/early-years/bilingual-quick-tips

THE LIST OF FIVE

No one tells you this, but once you have a school-age child you have to quit your job to become a full-time school–home liaison administrator. I'm joking, of course – but, blimey, there's a lot to remember, isn't there?

Firstly, you have to **LABEL** every single thing with their name. **EVERYTHING.** And even then half of their property will have disappeared by the end of the first term. Where does it all go? Ewan had a coat with his name written in it with a Sharpie pen and he came home one day in a coat with someone else's name in it and yet, two years on, his coat has not made a reappearance.

Also, the emails. **THE EMAILS!** I wish I'd set up a separate email account just for school emails. There are hundreds of them, not to mention the WhatsApp 'Reception Class' notifications pinging in, and the notes in their school bags. It feels like an administrative assault on your senses.

So when, two years into being a school parent, our school changed the policy on bringing in personal water bottles (thanks to COVID-19) it was just one step too many. I had it down before that. The reading record, the PE kit, washing the uniform (and speed ironing it with my hair straighteners at 8.25 a.m. in the morning!), the returning forms and signing of things. But now I **ALSO** had to remember to send them both in with a named, clean, full water bottle every day.

Obviously, in what has become quite a consistent pattern, I did pretty well for a few days and then one day forgot. I realized on the walk home that I'd sent my poor parched children into school without any form of refreshment. WHAT. A. FAIL.

I cursed myself the whole way home. *You idiot.* I should fill them up the night before and leave them by the door, shouldn't I? Except sometimes the call of the sofa and a chocolate orange of an evening is just too strong.

Then I paused. Hang on a minute. I had forgotten **ONE** thing. The list of stuff I had remembered was a **LOT** longer. The clean uniform, the form for flu sprays, updating the reading record, replying to the email about the school fair, telling the teacher about who was picking them up later. I'd remembered all that, but I was kicking myself about the one thing I had forgotten. And it's hardly like school isn't going to provide them with a drink all day, is it? There's that parental guilt once again, rearing its ugly head. The same *insert expletive* that rocks up into your brain to ask why they aren't sleeping through still at fourteen months when everyone else's baby is. Probably because you held them sleeping for too long, it says. Oh, piss off, guilt.

So instead I summon THE LIST OF FIVE to act as my guilt shield. When I've forgotten something, I immediately list five other things I **HAVE** done that day . . . and they can be anything – small or big.

1. Gave them breakfast.

2. Put on some mascara.

3. Got them to school on time.

4. Cleaned the dog poo off that shoe.

5. Loaded the dishwasher.

I did all that. Yes, I forgot the water bottle, but I remembered all those other things. So my recommendation for you when you also inevitably forget something is: don't sweat it. Think of your LIST OF FIVE and get on with your day. And, in the meantime, if someone could invent some sort of school uniform with an inbuilt homing chip I know we'd all hugely appreciate it.

READING

Scatter your books around the house and rotate them, changing them from month to month. If you have quite a few books, create different baskets or boxes in each room at a level your child can easily access. Anything new or different seems exciting to children, and changing the books might occasionally encourage them to pick one up instead of switching on the TV.

LEARNING TO READ

GHOTI

How do you pronounce this?

The answer is **FISH**. **GH** from enou**GH**, **O** from w**O**men and **TI** from sta**TI**on. **FISH**.

And this is why learning to read English is so flipping difficult!

One of the most significant things you will support your child with at home is learning to read. This is the cornerstone from which all other learning pivots. There is no feeling quite like the first time your kiddo sounds out those letters and blends them all together into a proper sentence. You can't believe they are reading. But it can be both equal amounts glorious and soul-destroying, because you can just as easily want to headbutt a wall when they've carefully sounded out the letters 'a-n-d' several times, yet your little one still looks at the picture on the page and follows it with . . . 'goat?' Because it's hard, isn't it? So let's break it down a bit.

There are three main elements to supporting your child with their reading at home that I will cover in this chapter: regular **READING** (pages 33–39), understanding **PHONICS** (pages 40–119) and learning **HIGH FREQUENCY WORDS** (pages 120–125).

READING

The first one is the most obvious: **READ WITH THEM**. All these things are beneficial when it comes to your child and reading:

- You reading **TO** them.
- You reading along **WITH** them.
- Listening to **AUDIOBOOKS** together and following along with the physical book in front of you.
- Them seeing **YOU** read for pleasure.
- Listening to **THEM** read.
- Taking it in **TURNS** to read pages or sentences.
- You reading almost a whole line but **PAUSING** to let them finish the final word.
- Reading the same books over and over until they've **MEMORIZED** them.
- Reading cereal packets, road signs, **MENUS**, instructions – anything at all.
- **ACTING** out a story from a book with some toys.
- Muting the TV and them reading the **SUBTITLES** of their favourite show!

BRINGING BOOKS HOME FROM SCHOOL

In some cases, when your child first starts bringing books home from school, you might open them and be surprised to find a perfectly nice story with absolutely no words in it. *What?! I thought we were supposed to be teaching them to read, not just looking at stuff on a page!*

It might seem strange that there are no words, when your child is supposed to be learning to read, but bear with it – because this is why:

- It gets them used to bringing a book home and starting that habit.

- For some children, who might not have books at home already, it gets them used to books, turning pages, holding them and flicking through them without the pressure of words.

- It means every single child can enjoy the book. So, even if they haven't started phonics yet, your child can talk about a story and enjoy the pictures.

- The wordless books get them familiar with characters they will be seeing and the style of books they will come across in school.

- Lots of wonderful stories have been told throughout history without any words. So it's a great way to introduce storytelling, as children will still be able to grasp what is happening just by looking at the pictures.

TIPS FOR WORDLESS BOOKS:

1. Ask your child about the images. Use open questions like '**WHAT CAN YOU SEE?**' or '**WHY DO YOU THINK THAT?**' – questions that mean they can't just give you 'yes' and 'no' answers.

2. If they struggle with this, try talking them through everything you can see on the page and explain what you think it might mean. For example: 'I can see the trees are bent over and have swirly lines near them – I think that means it must be windy.'

3. Ask your child to predict what they think is going to happen before turning the pages, even when you've read it a few times and they know. It's good practice to develop their storytelling skills.

4. Talk about all the different bits of the book: the title, the author, the illustrator, the page numbers, even the contents page – anything that interests them!

5. Re-tell the story afterwards. Can they remember what happened? Talk about your favourite pages and why you liked them.

FIRST WORDS

Hurrah! Words at last! you might be thinking as your child proudly brings home a reading book. *Let's read.* But several minutes later you're thinking you need a lie-down in a dark room and wondering if perhaps you can outsource this job to a grandparent.

Yep, this bit can sometimes be a bit . . . how shall we put it? Testing. Typical things that can happen during this first part of learning to read include guessing words or sounding out the letters correctly but blending them together backwards (for example, p-a-t . . . TAP!). It can seem like they're never going to get it. But this is completely normal for a child learning to read. Their brains are working overtime. They're trying to remember the sounds the letters make, then hold those sounds in their head and remember the order they went in. Then, while doing all the remembering, they have to blend them together into a word that sounds familiar. It's a lot to ask. Imagine me showing you ancient hieroglyphics and expecting you to be able to read them after a few goes?

So what can we do to help with this process? Well, mostly just be patient and keep going. But here are a few tips to help you get there with a shred of your inner peace still intact:

- You read the book to them first, and use your finger to follow the text.
- Show them how you split up the words, then sound out the letters and **BLEND** them in an exaggerated way. 'This is **d-o-g** – I wonder what it says? Let's blend those sounds together, shall we?'
- When you blend, do it slowly at first and then get faster and faster: '**d-ooooo-g, d-ooo-g, d-o-g, dog**!'
- Let your little one read the single sounds out loud but you repeat and then blend for them until the sounds make a word.
- Play some blending games like Puzzle Blending (page 78) or Extra Silly Soup (page 83)!

Some of Ewan and Flo's favourite books don't have words in. We have a few books, like *You Choose*, which are mainly detailed pictures and you choose what you like in each picture. These sorts of books are fantastic for speech and language. The book doesn't always have to be a written story, especially if your child has a short attention span for wordy books.

TWIDDLY BITS

There are lots of things in books that aren't letters but we still need to understand. Things like exclamation marks. Upon seeing one, children will often initially insist it is an upside down '**i**' and so make an '**ih**' sound! You can't really blame them – after all, letters are just squiggles on a page really, aren't they? So of course they could be upside down! The best things to do when they spot something like this is to give them a straightforward and simple explanation and follow it up by demonstrating it in a sentence. Here are my examples:

? **THIS IS A QUESTION MARK.** If it's at the end of a sentence, it means the sentence is asking a question. 'Can I play with you?' would have a question mark at the end.

! **THIS IS AN EXCLAMATION MARK.** When we see this, it means the word needs to be said with some extra effort. Often it's shouted or said loudly like 'Watch out!'

“ ” **THESE ARE SPEECH MARKS.** They show when someone is speaking. So if the sentence was *Mummy said, "Let's go to the park."*, the 'Let's go to the park' part would have speech marks before the word *Let's* and after the word *park*. (Books for young children usually use double speech marks to help children differentiate between apostrophes and the speech marks at the end of speech. As they get older, they'll come across books that use single speech marks instead.)

' **THIS IS AN APOSTROPHE.** It has lots of uses. In the word *they're*, for example, it's used in place of a letter. So it really means 'they are' but 'they're' is a quicker way of saying and writing it, so we use an apostrophe to show a letter is missing in this word. I've got some fun apostrophe games on pages 116–117.

You get the idea. Explain it clearly using simple language your child will understand and always give working examples afterwards. Let them try to think of an example if they like.

The Oxford Owl website has free ebooks that are ideal for early readers: home.oxfordowl.co.uk

READING LEVELS

When your child is given books to take home, they are often of a particular level or colour that matches your child's confidence levels. Teachers assess this regularly, reading with your child to see how they are getting on, and moving them up the levels when they know they are ready. Your child could go through a few levels in a matter of weeks or they might stay at one level for months and months. It depends on the child, the amount they are reading, how easily they are grasping phonics and their confidence levels.

Reading-book levels can be a playing field for competitiveness between classmates, and even the grown-ups. Although this can be positive, as sometimes a child wanting to be on the same level as their friend might be motivated to read more, at other times it can cause unhelpful pressure. See more about comparison on page 14.

Just bear in mind that the speed and fluency of your child reading the words in a book isn't the only thing they are assessed on. Teachers also might ask them:

- what a word or phrase means
- to retell the events of the story after they've read the book
- to understand how and why the characters might feel the way they do
- to look for clues in the text to predict the next part of the story, or to understand previous parts
- to use expression in their reading, so speaking with emphasis when there is an exclamation mark or changing their tone when they can see someone is speaking

If your child can read a book but doesn't really know what happens in the story, then they won't be moved up a level, no matter how confident they seem. We can help with **COMPREHENSION** at home, before they even start to read themselves, with these simple things:

- Take your time when reading together to pause so both of you can ask questions.
- Refer to pictures as you read, and explain how we can look for story clues in both the pictures and the words we are hearing and saying.
- Ask them to predict what they think might happen next.
- Take it in turns to re-tell bits of the story when you've finished a book.
- Compare your favourite part of the story with theirs and both talk about why you like those bits.
- Comment on the emotions of characters. For example, '*Oooh! How do you think he's feeling now? Why do you think that?*'

Also bear in mind that schools have a LOT of books. Some of the resources might be years old, and the words your child has on the page might seem beyond them, or the colour band on the spine might not match the standard of the other books they've read. If it's too difficult for them to attempt, just read it to your child instead and pop a note in their bag to the teacher explaining that they found it too tricky to read. Likewise, if you're not sure about the book they've been given because it seems too simple, let them enjoy the ease of it and return it with a note. Stickers fall off, books get put into the wrong boxes and some have been around since your own parents were at school. Don't sweat it. Just do your best to read with them, or to them, with whatever is sent home and let the teacher know if you have any queries.

BUT I DON'T WANT TO

If you do any reading of any kind regularly with your kiddos, then you are already quite magnificent! And yet sometimes we get stuck. There will be times while learning to read when your child might find it really difficult. They might not want to read today. They will perhaps dig their heels in and protest that it's too hard. When Ewan did this, I found it one of the most challenging things to not get frustrated about: knowing that he was making good progress and yet suddenly didn't want to do it any more. Argh! Your mind starts playing tricks, and you believe they will fall behind their classmates if they don't stick to a rigid reading schedule. It's easy for the pressure to creep in.

If your child is feeling this way, please don't panic. Try some of these ideas instead:

- Stop reading for a little while. Have a rest for a couple of weeks.
- Read to them. Your child doesn't have to read a full book from school daily to make progress. Sometimes just listening to you read, as you follow the words with your finger, can be massively helpful too.
- Visit a library, bookshop or charity shop and let them choose a book they like the look of for you to read together at home.
- Encourage a love of stories: talk about stories that you love, and try to rekindle the enjoyment and fun that can be found in any kind of story. Dig out books that are their old favourites and leave them where your little ones can see them to tempt them into hearing a story you know they love.
- When they are feeling a bit more confident about reading, encourage them slowly. Perhaps, when you're reading aloud, pause at words you know that they know and see if they'd like to read them.
- Say you'll read a page each.

Likewise, if you (or your partner) isn't a confident reader or feels daunted by text on a page, make it simpler. The key to unlocking words is to break them down, and try to make it as fun as you can. That is true for both you and your children, so if you're finding it confusing, tell them so and find a way to work around it together. Speed is not of the essence here. It's about little and often. So turn reading into a game! The rest of this chapter is full of games and ideas to take words out of books and to mess about with them, so reading becomes easy and joyful. So let's start with **PHONICS** and get playing!

If you're struggling to encourage them to read, just sit quietly in a comfy corner of your sofa with a book. I guarantee within minutes you'll have a child on your lap asking what you're doing! They can't resist!

PHONICS

One of the first blog posts I ever wrote was called 'WTAF is Phonics?' As a teaching assistant, I was often called upon to deliver phonics sessions to a small group of children, which was one of my favourite things to teach. However, there was a time, while I was a school volunteer before my training, when I heard a child say they'd spotted a digraph in a book – and I remember thinking . . .

'WHAT ON EARTH IS HE ON ABOUT?'

I had to sneak back into the classroom one break time to frantically look up digraphs and then discovered PHONICS – a whole new way of learning to read! The reason that schools teach phonics is because it's a way to break down the English language into easily learnable chunks. Phonics is simply teaching the kids the SOUNDS the letters in our alphabet make in words, sometimes as a single letter or sometimes as a group of letters. (There are twenty-six letters but forty-four sounds! I'll get to those later.) This method is designed to make it simpler for children. When it works, it can give children huge confidence very quickly as they break down words into sounds that they are familiar with. It gives them the 'code' to unlock reading and writing. In this section I am going to explain phonics by introducing its main points, and by then going through its six phases with games and resource pages to match.

BUT IT'S ALL SO COMPLICATED, ISN'T IT?

The thing about phonics that I first discovered is that everything about it seems way more complicated than it is. Strange jargon is used, and the format seems a world away from what we were taught in school. But actually phonics is incredibly similar in lots of ways, and the jargon is just that: jargon. Once you know a few of the terms, you can get the hang of it incredibly quickly.

So, to get that out of the way, I've written a glossary for all the phonics terms over the next couple of pages for you to refer to if you ever find yourself thinking, as I once did:

'WHAT ON EARTH ARE THEY ON ABOUT?'

PHONICS:

Phon is Greek for 'sound'. The system of phonics is about learning to read and write through the sounds we hear when we speak and how they are represented by the letters on a page.

GRAPHEME:

This is the letter or letters that represent the sound as seen written on a page.

PHONEME:

This is the sound we hear, made by one letter, or two, or sometimes even three. One unit of sound is called a phoneme. There are forty-four phonemes in the English language. There are more sounds than letters in the alphabet.

GRAPHEME PHONEME CORRESPONDENCE (GPC):

This means matching up graphemes and phonemes. So matching the letters on the page to the sounds we hear, and vice versa. Basically READING!

CVC WORDS:

These are words that consist of a Consonant-Vowel-Consonant, like **sat**, **mop** and **pin**. As the phases go on, you might see CVCC words (like **push**) or CCVCC words (such as **trick**). The C and V always stand for consonant and vowel.

DIGRAPH:

These are two letters that make one sound (**di** means 'two'). For example, the **a** and **i** in the word **rain** (r-ai-n). The **ai** is a digraph, two letters making one /ay/ sound.

SPLIT DIGRAPH:

These are two letters that make one sound when they are seen together but are split up in the written word. So, for example, in the word **made**, the **a** and **e** make the /ay/ sound, but they are split up by the **d**.

An example of a split digraph:

makes the /ay/ sound

TRIGRAPH:

These are three letters that make one sound (**tri** means 'three'). For example, the letters **igh** together in the word **light** (l-igh-t) make the sound /eye/.

PREFIX:

A letter or letters added to the beginning of a word to change its meaning. For example, using the prefix re- (meaning 'again') to change the word **apply** to become **reapply**.

SUFFIX:

A group of letters added to the end of a word to change its meaning. For example, adding the suffix -ed (for the past tense), so **walk** becomes **walked**.

BLENDING:

Putting the individual sounds together to make a word. The sounds **b-r-ai-n** are blended to make **brain**. Both segmenting (see right) and blending can be done orally (by speaking the sounds aloud), so sometimes you might also hear the term 'oral segmenting', or 'oral blending', which is done first before children attempt to read or write.

SEGMENTING:

Splitting up a word into its sounds, so **brain** is segmented as **b-r-ai-n**

SLASHES:

Sometimes sounds are represented like this: **/ay/** The forward slashes represent the sound we hear or say. So you might see **ea** with **/ee/** next to it, because **/ee/** represents the sound you hear in the word **meat**. The slashes tell you the sound those two letters are making, because there might be another way you could also hear or say them, such as **/eh/** in **head**. Same letters but with alternative sounds.

There's more on alternative sounds on page 108.

/ed/

SOUND BUTTONS:

These are dots or dashes under words or letters to help children know whether to make one sound or two when they see them. For example, a digraph would have a line underneath it to show the child to say the letters together as one sound. But the other letters might have dots if they are single letters that represent a sound each.

fish

shell

sea

IMPORTANT! YOU DON'T NEED TO MEMORIZE ALL THIS TO HELP YOUR KIDS WITH PHONICS!

A BIT MORE ABOUT BLENDING AND SEGMENTING

Here's a diagram that I often use to help others to understand blending and segmenting:

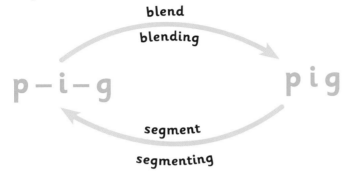

CAN WE STILL SING THE ALPHABET SONG?

Short answer? YES! Children need to know both the letter **NAMES** – **/ay/ (a)**, **/bee/ (b)**, **/see/ (c)**, **/dee/ (d)** that we sing in the alphabet song – as well as the **SOUNDS** the letters make, which they learn through phonics. So if your child sees a **c** and says 'That's a **/see/**' we would reply that they are correct, and we might then follow it up with 'And what sound does it make?' Your child might then reply 'cuh' as in *cot*, which would also be correct.

A good example is to think of an animal like a cow. It is called a cow, and it goes moo. We wouldn't say it's called a moo. This is why it's useful not to refer to letters solely as the sounds they make, because lots of letters can make multiple sounds as we will find out in Phase 5 (page 100). Are you still with me?! Or have you nodded off? I wouldn't blame you at all!

This can be tricky, I know. If you're more of an aural or visual learner, I've also got a video of me explaining all this on my website: **fiveminutemum.com**

LOWER CASE OR UPPER CASE?

As I mentioned in the Using this Book section (page 7), children need to gradually get to know both upper-case and lower-case letters. However, when we teach phonics sounds, we mostly use lower-case letters simply because they are what we see most often when we read.

There are some games on pages 63–65 to help children understand the cases and when to use them. When explaining capital letters, make sure you use the same sounds as for lower-case letters. Explaining that names have capital letters at the beginning is also a useful thing for a child to understand.

NONSENSE WORDS

A big part of phonics is not just learning to read words we know but also reading nonsense words. 'WHY?' I hear you ask. Why indeed. Well, the reason for this is because nonsense words can still help children to practise their phonics. Whether they are sounding out c-a-t-ch or c-a-l-sh, they are using the same skills.

Playing around with nonsense words is also useful because some children might be very good at using pictures as clues to memorize words. So a kiddo might see the word *cat* alongside a picture of a cat, then the next time they see the word *cat* they remember that the word means cat; they don't need to sound out the letters. This obviously is fantastic but, when it comes to reading new words, this memory skill won't necessarily help them, especially if there are no pictures to accompany the words. Our kids need to have phonics knowledge as well to be able to recognize words, so that they can decode more complicated and longer words later on. For games with nonsense words in, skip to Buried Treasure on page 75 and Puzzle Blending on pages 78 – 79.

LET'S ALL DO IT DIFFERENTLY . . . !

Crikey. I've covered loads over the last few pages, so let's crack on with explaining phonics in a nice straightforward way. Oh, except, no, we can't . . . Because there are actually quite a few different programmes for teaching phonics, and each approaches the method slightly differently.

The one I have found to be used most commonly is part of the Primary National Strategy from the UK's governmental Department for Education and Skills. It is called *Letters and Sounds: Principles and Practice of High-Quality Phonics*. Catchy title, innit? This is the programme I always used in teaching, and the one that I'll be guiding you through in this book. You can find a copy of it online at www.gov.uk/education/phonics, although – fair warning – it's pretty yawn-inducing!

There are other phonics strategies and teaching methods being used in schools, such as Read Write Inc. or Jolly Phonics. They don't differ hugely, but it does mean that your school might have its own way of doing it. So, although I can give you a general explanation of things that will be useful to everyone no matter what method your children's school follows, you might come across things that I haven't covered here that your school uses, or some terminology in this book might sound unfamiliar because your child (and their school) does it differently.

Don't worry! This won't matter with the games I've outlined in this chapter, but my advice to you is to always be led by your child and the school they are in. Quite often schools offer sessions for parents on phonics, and I would wholeheartedly suggest you go along if at all possible. It's a great time to question the teachers and make sure you fully understand what they will be doing in the classroom.

Even though I had taught phonics a few years before, I still went to the session when Ewan started school, and sat on a tiny chair for half an hour to listen to what his teachers said, because I found the reminder so helpful and because you never know when the government will decide to change it all again! Plus, you can smile encouragingly at other parents and suss out the ones who might be up for a coffee or pub bevvy later!

WHAT NEXT?

I hope through this introduction I've covered some of the questions you had around phonics. The next part of this chapter is going to take you through phonics, one phase at a time. Each phase will include:

- an introduction covering the main things that your little one will learn during that phase
- some games to play
- a resources page, which will have all the sounds and words introduced during that phase (if it has any) set out as flash cards

If you think the phases seem a bit random, it's because they really are! But don't forget: as someone who is just supporting from home, it isn't up to us to TEACH this stuff or comprehensively understand it. We just need to roughly get it so we can crack on with playing some fun five-minute games to get familiar with what our kiddos are learning. So let's go!

PHASE 1

This is the first phase of phonics (or just the first bit if your kiddo's school follows a phonics programme that doesn't use phases). It's very straightforward: it's basically about listening to, and identifying, sounds. Children at school or nursery will be encouraged to play lots of games where they have to guess what is making the sound, whether it be animal noises, musical instruments or environmental noises. Any sounds will do!

You can easily support this through play at home, and you probably already do. Here are a few ideas, though, you might want to try:

- **MAKE DIFFERENT NOISES** and move your body to represent loud and quiet. So big steps for bangs on a drum or saucepan, and little tiptoes for a gentle jingling bell.

- **MAKE AN ANIMAL SOUND** and get them to guess which animal it is.

- **HOLD FIVE OBJECTS** behind your back that make a noise. Hit or move one and see if your child can guess which one made the noise.

- **SING ANY KIND OF NURSERY RHYME** that has a sound action such as clap, and change it each time to stamp, or click, or whoosh.

- **ASK YOUR CHILD TO CLOSE THEIR EYES,** then move around the room, making a noise with something – a box of dried pasta works well. Can they point to where they hear it and tell you how it sounds different in different parts of the room?

- **PLAY I SPY** using rhyming clues. So 'I spy with my little eye something that sounds like socks' and the answer could be 'box'. Can they hear the rhyme?

- **PLAY ODD ONE OUT** – say three items (two that rhyme and one that doesn't) and see if your child can tell you the odd one out. So, for example, 'I've got a spoon, a moon and a lamp. Which is the odd one out?' You can do this with sounds at the start of words too. So you might have a fork, a fox and a banana. Which one is the odd one out?

- **SING A SONG YOU KNOW AND ASK THEM TO SING IT IN DIFFERENT WAYS.** Can they sing it in a squeaky voice? How about a loud booming voice? Can they (or you!) sing it like a sheep would?

- **MIRROR PLAY** – draw a circle on a mirror with a whiteboard marker (or lipstick, if you like!) to represent a sound button. Sit in front of the mirror with your child and 'press' the button. Make a different sound each time and watch your faces. So you could oink or hiss, sing 'ding-dong', shout your name or even blow a raspberry. Let them change the sounds too, but they have to press the button!

WHAT WE SAY COUNTS

For all phonics phases, it's really helpful to sometimes break up words you might say often into sounds. So you could say, 'Let's put on your coat – **c-oa-t**' or 'These steps are steep – **s-t-ee-p**!' Or your child might notice a rhyme in something; for example, you could say, 'Please don't squeeze the cheese.' You'd follow this up by highlighting the rhyme: '**Pl-eeee-se** don't **squ-eeee-ze** the **ch-eeee-se**!' All these funny little things we notice and say in speech, believe it or not, are helping your little one when it comes to learning to read and write.

SYLLABLE CLAPS

Something that is fun to do is encouraging kids to guess from syllable clapping. So, for example, at snack time they might have the choice between a banana and an apple (or Monster Munch and Quavers, I ain't judging!) or any choice that has a different number of syllables in. You say they have to answer in claps what they would like, then you demonstrate the options. Point at a banana and do three claps – for **ba-na-na** – then point at the apple and do two claps (**app-le**). Then they reply with claps. You can say the words as you clap too, so they understand what they are clapping out if they're confused.

If you have two children with a different number of syllables in their names, you could revert to clapping sometimes instead of shouting their names a thousand times! Unfortunately I didn't think of this when I named Ewan and Florence. Same number of syllables – damn.

PHASE 2

This second phase, typically for ages four to five, is where we actually start to introduce letters (graphemes) and teach the children the sounds (phonemes) they make – except in phonics we don't start with the letters at the beginning of the alphabet. We start with what, in teaching, is often referred to as 'satpin' (a shorthand way to talk about the first sounds introduced in phonics). The group of letters opposite is usually slowly introduced when children start school, around the age of four, over the course of many weeks. Some phonics programmes might vary the order slightly, but they're all similar.

Here are the first letters your little ones will learn, alongside some notes on the pronunciation, which is the most important bit of phonics.

These sounds and more example words are on the resources page at the end of this phase (page 68) if you want to make your own flash cards.

You can also go to **fiveminutemum.com** to see a video of me saying all these sounds.

s	the **s** in **sun** – pronounced **/sss/** like a hiss
a	the **a** in **apple**
t	the **t** in **tin**
p	the **p** in **pot**
i	the **i** in **ink**
n	the **n** in **sun** – pronounced **/nnn/**
m	the **m** in **mum** – pronounced **/mmm/** like a **hum**
d	the **d** in **dog**
g	the **g** in **gap**
o	the **o** in **octopus**
c	the **c** in **cat**
k	the **k** in **king**
ck	the **ck** in **kick** – children learn that both letters together make one short **/cuh/** sound
e	the **e** in **egg**
u	the **u** in **up**
r	the **r** in **red** – pronounced **/rrr/** like a **roar**
h	the **h** in **hat**
b	the **b** in **bug**

Some words, like **puff**, **hill** and **kiss**, have a pattern of the same letter being used twice, but a double letter doesn't mean saying the sound twice:

f, ff	the **f** in **fish** – both make the sound **/fff/** (like when you're about to swear and realize you can't because there's a small child in the room!)
l, ll	the **l** in **lion** – both make a sound like **/ul/**
s, ss	the **ss** in **miss** – both make the **/sss/** sound like a hiss

The /uh/ in /muh/ and /suh/ is called a SCHWA in technical terms, in case you ever need to know this for a quiz question – because, as parents, we sure as heck don't really need to!

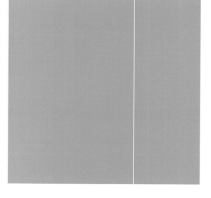

SAY IT LOUD, SAY IT CLEAR

The biggest thing to remember when chatting about these letters with your kids is not to add the /uh/ sound on the end when you say them. So the sound for **s** is /sss/. And the sound for **m** is /mmm/. Not /suh/ or /muh/ like we were perhaps taught. If you get that down, you are all good. Basically, if you are unsure of the sound a letter is supposed to make, think of a simple word with that letter in and the smallest, most simplified sound it makes when you're saying it. So say 'sat' out loud slowly and you will hear the /sss/ at the start. That's what you're after. You can find lots of videos online of people demonstrating the correct way to say all these sounds.

At this point, we are mainly encouraging our kids to read the letters and match the sounds they make orally. Some children might like to write them down, and there are games that teachers will play where they 'draw' the letters in the air with their fingers, or write it in sand or on to a tray of shaving foam. However, don't worry about letter formation at this stage; it's more important for your kiddos to concentrate on matching letters they see with the sounds and vice versa.

YOU PLAY TOO

Your kiddo won't get it all right away, of course. So how do we go about learning to match those letters and sounds? We play games with them! Don't forget: often the first time you play games with letters, YOU will be doing all the work. You'll be matching them up and saying the sounds, and your little one might be listening or even seem completely uninterested. The aim here is to simply keep going, little and often, exposing them to the letters and sounds as frequently as you can in a light-hearted and fun way. So the next few pages are filled with games to do just that!

Some more examples of words to use are on the Phase 2 resources page 71.

SOUND CHECK

When children are first learning these sounds, it's brilliant to give them lots of examples of words where the sound is heard at the start of the word, so they can hear it represented clearly (some examples are on page 71). However, don't forget it's also good practice to listen out for the sound in the middle or at the end of words too. Here's a quick game to practise that.

GRAB:

- paper
- pen
- flash card for whatever sound you are learning

TO SET UP . . .

Write down some sentences that include words with the sound you are learning. The sound can appear at the beginning, middle or end of the word. Here are some examples:

For **s** —— The snake hisses when Miss Smith tries to kiss it on the speedy bus.

For **a** —— The ant and the cat went to find an apple with a map.

For **t** —— Mrs Turner went to a shop and got some turnips for Aunt Betty.

For **p** —— Peter Piper saw an ape on top of a flower pot, eating a grape.

For **i** —— If you dig with a pick, you can make an igloo.

For **n** —— Nancy was very naughty when she went on the bus to nursery.

TO PLAY . . .

1. Give your child the flash card and remind them of the sound the letter makes.
2. Tell them you're going to say a silly sentence and they're going to be your sound checker.
3. Say the sentence out loud: first at a normal pace, then again a bit slower.
4. Next, tell your child that you're going to say the sentence again one word at a time and if they think they can hear the sound on the flash card, they have to hold it up.
5. If they get it right, celebrate! If not, say, 'Hmm, I'm not sure. Let's listen again.' And repeat the words to see if they can hear the sound on a second attempt.

FLASH CARD MATCH-UP

Florence loves games to be fast and frantic. Unlike her big brother who prefers order and calm, Flo loves a whirlwind to surround everything she does. In order to help her learn some of her phonics sounds, when she came home with a keyring of her 'key sounds' from school, I created this fast and furious game, which she adored because it got faster and crazier until we were both lying on the floor laughing.

GRAB:

- 2 sets of letter flash cards, with letters matching the phonics sounds to be learned

TO SET UP . . .

1. Turn one set face down and spread them all out.
2. Gather the second set in a pile, keeping the cards face down.

TO PLAY . . .

1. Ask your child to choose a card from the second set (as in the photo opposite).
2. Encourage them to say the sound on the card they've selected.
3. Then say '**GO**' and you both have to turn over the first set of cards that are spread out as fast as you can, one at a time, racing against each other, until someone finds the matching card.
4. Whoever found the matching card keeps it.
5. Turn the first set of cards back over, so they're face down again and you can't see what's on them, then mix them up.
6. Ask your child to choose the next card from the second set and repeat. You can take turns with revealing the next card, or it can be the person who got the previous matching card.
7. The one with the most cards at the end wins.

TEDDY BEARS' SOUND PICNIC

Some children absolutely love role play. It's a funny one because as an adult it can be really hard to get into the groove with role play. Pretending to play 'mummies and daddies' isn't quite as fun when you already are a parent and realize it involves a lot more than just putting your baby into a cot to get them to go to sleep! But nonetheless kids can get a lot out of playing this way, so sometimes we have to just grin and bear it . . . (See what I did there?!)

GRAB:

- 5 teddy bears or soft toys
- a small blanket or tea towel
- some bowls or plates, and cups (toy or plastic)
- 5 food items (real or toy food) that are easily sounded out, for example, jam, cheese, cake, apple, pear, ham, fish
- paper and a pen

TO SET UP . . .

1. Lay out the soft toys around the picnic blanket.
2. Write the five food items on bits of paper, with sound buttons too if you like (see page 68), and give one to each toy.

TO PLAY . . .

1. Each toy has an order for the picnic.
2. Ask your child to get their order and bring it over to the pile of food.
3. You will tell them what the order says but only in letter sounds. So you might say: 'This teddy bear would like some **j-a-m**.' Your child has to listen carefully to the sounds and try to hear the word, so that they're learning to blend sounds to make a word.
4. Once they get it right, they can take the item for their picnic. Help them, if they're struggling, by blending the sounds together for them.
5. Keep going until each order is done. Then swap over and let your child take the orders and attempt to make the sounds if they like.

You can obviously play this game without the swiping arms too. Kids are happy to just chuck beanbags at things!

You can play this outside by chalking the letters on patio tiles or the pavement. Instead of keeping the letter, the player crosses out the letter and writes their initial next to it. The winner is whoever has crossed out the most letters.

WRECKING BALL

What child isn't going to love a game called this?! It also used to be Florence's nickname as a baby because Ewan would carefully set up all his train tracks and we would take bets as to how long it would be before she attempted to destroy his hard work! Fun for all the family! Now, though, we play in a different way. Those days seem long gone. Mad how fast they go, isn't it?

GRAB:

- cards with the letters or sounds you want to learn on them
- a beanbag (if you don't have one, fill a bag or sock with dry rice and tie it with an elastic band)

TO SET UP . . .

1. Lay the cards out in a space, letter side up.
2. All players sit in a circle around the cards. The youngest player is Player 1.

TO PLAY . . .

1. Player 1 gets a turn to throw the beanbag into the air over the cards. The idea is to get the beanbag to land on a card.
2. However, the other players each get one 'wrecking ball' swipe through the air to attempt to knock the beanbag away from the cards before it lands. The trick is to try to perfectly time your arm swiping across the play space!
3. You only get one arm swipe for each go, and you can play your 'wrecking ball' at any moment. Just make sure if there are multiple players that they're standing far enough apart so their arms won't clash.
4. If the beanbag lands on a card, Player 1 says which sound is on that card. They then keep that card. If it doesn't land on a card, the beanbag is passed to the next player.
5. Keep taking turns to throw the beanbag until all the cards have been won. The player with the most cards wins.

You can also play pairs. Lay the cards face down and take it in turns to select two and see if they match. If they do, you keep them. Keep playing until all the cards are gone. Make sure you say the sounds your letters make out loud as you play!

SOUND SNAP

You are probably beginning to realize why on page 7 I recommend making your own sets of flash cards! If you have a few sets of cards with letters on you can play endless games. This is the kind of game that is so simple to play in five minutes, but if played often will have maximum impact.

GRAB:

■ 2 identical sets of cards with the sounds that need to be learned

TO SET UP . . .

1. Shuffle the cards and split them into two even piles: one for you, one for your child.

TO PLAY . . .

1. Just play **SNAP!** At the same time, turn over the top card on each of your stacks and place it in a central spot between you both.
2. If they are the same, shout '**SNAP!**' and put your hand over them.
3. The first person to do this has to say the sound the letters make. Once they've said it, they keep all the turned-over cards in the middle, and add them to the bottom of their stack.
4. Keep playing until one player runs out of cards and the other player is the winner.

PEG IT

Wooden pegs are really handy to have. You can get bags of pegs in supermarkets and pound shops, and they can be used for lots of play. The great thing about pegs is that the hand muscles required to open and shut them are the same as the ones required to write, so when children play with pegs they are building those crucial little muscles. Peg play, especially with letters, is a superb alternative to writing if your child is reluctant to pick up a pencil. So here are a couple of ideas to try:

GAME 1

GRAB:

- a bag of pegs
- a marker pen
- 5 items which each start with a different letter: for example, a book, a fork, an umbrella, a scarf and a tissue

TO SET UP . . .

1. Write the first letter of each item on a peg and leave them nearby.

TO PLAY . . .

1. Say the sound the letter makes on each peg and then say the name of the items.
2. Can your child put the peg on the correct item?

You can play this with more complicated sounds as your child progresses through the phases. For example, can your child identify the /th/ sound in cloth? The /ck/ sound in jacket or /oo/ sound in spoon?

GAME 2

GRAB:

- a piece of cardboard
- a pen
- some pegs

TO SET UP . . .

1. Write letters in capitals along the edge of the piece of card.
2. Write matching lower-case letters on the pegs.

TO PLAY . . .

1. Ask your child to match up the correct lower-case and capital letters.
2. Hang the cardboard high up so they can just reach, so the pegging is more fun.

You could even write all the letters of the alphabet on the pegs, and keep a set handy to make words later, as your little one goes through the phonics phases.

If you have some plain connecting bricks of any kind, writing letters on them is a great way to extend their play use. You can then use them for spellings too.

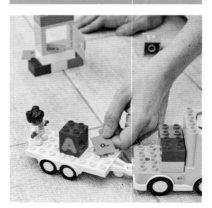

CAPITAL IDEA

A wee while ago the people at LEGO® asked me to come up with some ideas for their new DUPLO® sets. Obviously I was more than happy to, because DUPLO® is always part of our regular play and the new blocks had letters on! What could be better? So I came up with this game to play with Flo one afternoon. Now, when it comes to phonics, the letters make the same sound regardless of whether they are upper- or lower-case letters. We tend to focus on lower-case letters as these are what we see more of when we read, but upper-case (capitals) are important to know too. Here's a game to help our kids know the difference between the two.

GRAB:

- anything with capital letters on, such as flash cards or blocks
- pen
- paper
- scissors
- something to use as a postbox (we built ours out of DUPLO® but you could use anything with a little door, or you can make one from a box)
- a toy vehicle with some sort of carriage

TO SET UP . . .

1. Lay out the capital letters around a room.
2. Create your postbox, either out of toy blocks or cardboard.
3. Write matching lower-case letters on the paper and cut them out individually – pop one into the 'letter box' and leave the rest nearby.
4. Set up the vehicle close to you.

TO PLAY . . .

1. Say that there is a letter in the letter box with an order on it for your child to collect.
2. They open the box and identify the letter, saying the sound it makes.
3. Next, they pop the order into the vehicle's carriage and take it around the room, looking for the matching letter.
4. Explain to your child that the order is in lower case and the one they need is upper case. Help them at first if it's tricky.
5. Once they find the correct upper-case letter, ask them to bring it back to you, so you can collect all the orders.
6. Then you pop a new lower-case letter into the letter box for them to collect.

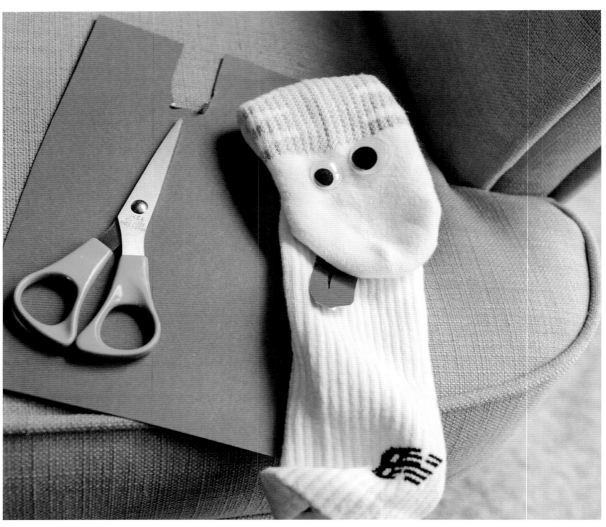

OLD FIVE-MINUTE GAMES REVISITED

Before we move on to the next phase, I want to revisit some games from my website that also appeared in my previous book, *Give Me Five*. I played these with my two to introduce them to letters. For these games, I didn't begin at home with 'satpin'; instead I used the letters of their names, because they were of interest to them. Don't feel you have to rigidly stick to phonics phases at home; as always, be led by your child's curiosity. Here's a recap of some of those games, updated a little, that I found to be really useful for this phonics phase:

TARGET PRACTICE: Write the letters on something and fire things at them. Shout out the sounds the letters make when you hit them. Versions we have played include:

- Wet sponges splatting chalk letters on a fence.
- Foam bullets launched at letters written on bits of paper stuck to walls.
- Kicking balls at letters hung on outside goals or washing lines.
- Water balloons splatting letters written in chalk on the pavement.
- Throwing balls at buckets with letters stuck on the front of them.

TREASURE HUNT: Grab any form of letters and hide them around a room or the garden. As your little one returns the letters (you could collect them in a bucket), you and your child can identify them and the sound they make. A prize at the end always makes it worthwhile!

THE HUNGRY PUPPET: Grab a hand puppet or a sock, lay out some letters and tell your child that the puppet is hungry. You say the letter sound and your child needs to feed the puppet the correct letter to match the sound. The puppet spits out the wrong ones and makes silly 'yuck' noises.

ALPHABET CAR PARK: On a piece of card draw a grid and fill the spaces of the grid with letters. Now lay out some cars. Say a word that has a letter sound from the grid, and see if your child can park the car in the space in the grid to match the sound.

RUB IT OUT: Write letters on to any surface that's wipeable: for example, whiteboard markers on a window or mirror, in shaving foam on a tile wall, or in chalk on a board. Then shout a sound out and see if your kiddo can rub out the letter that matches it.

PHASE 2 RESOURCES

Here are the sounds set out for you to use as flash cards for games or as a reference point. The dots and dashes under the letters are sound buttons (see page 42 for an explanation).

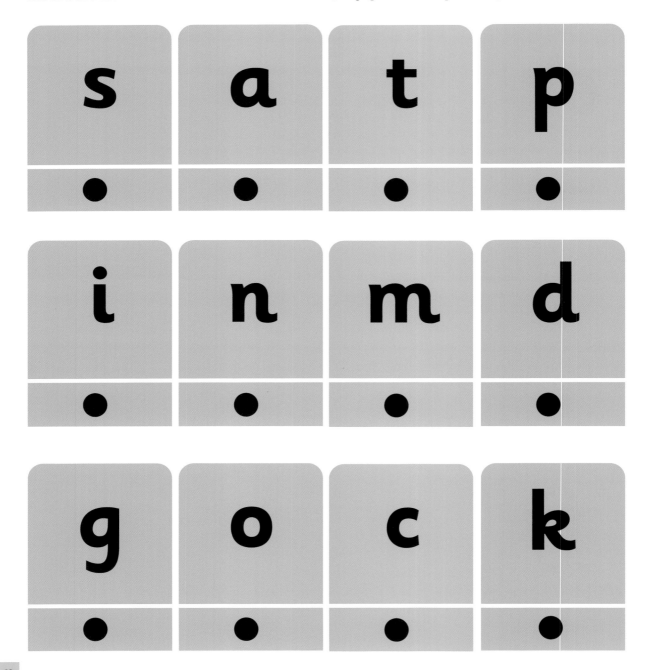

On page 70, I've also given you an example of how you could create your own flash cards.

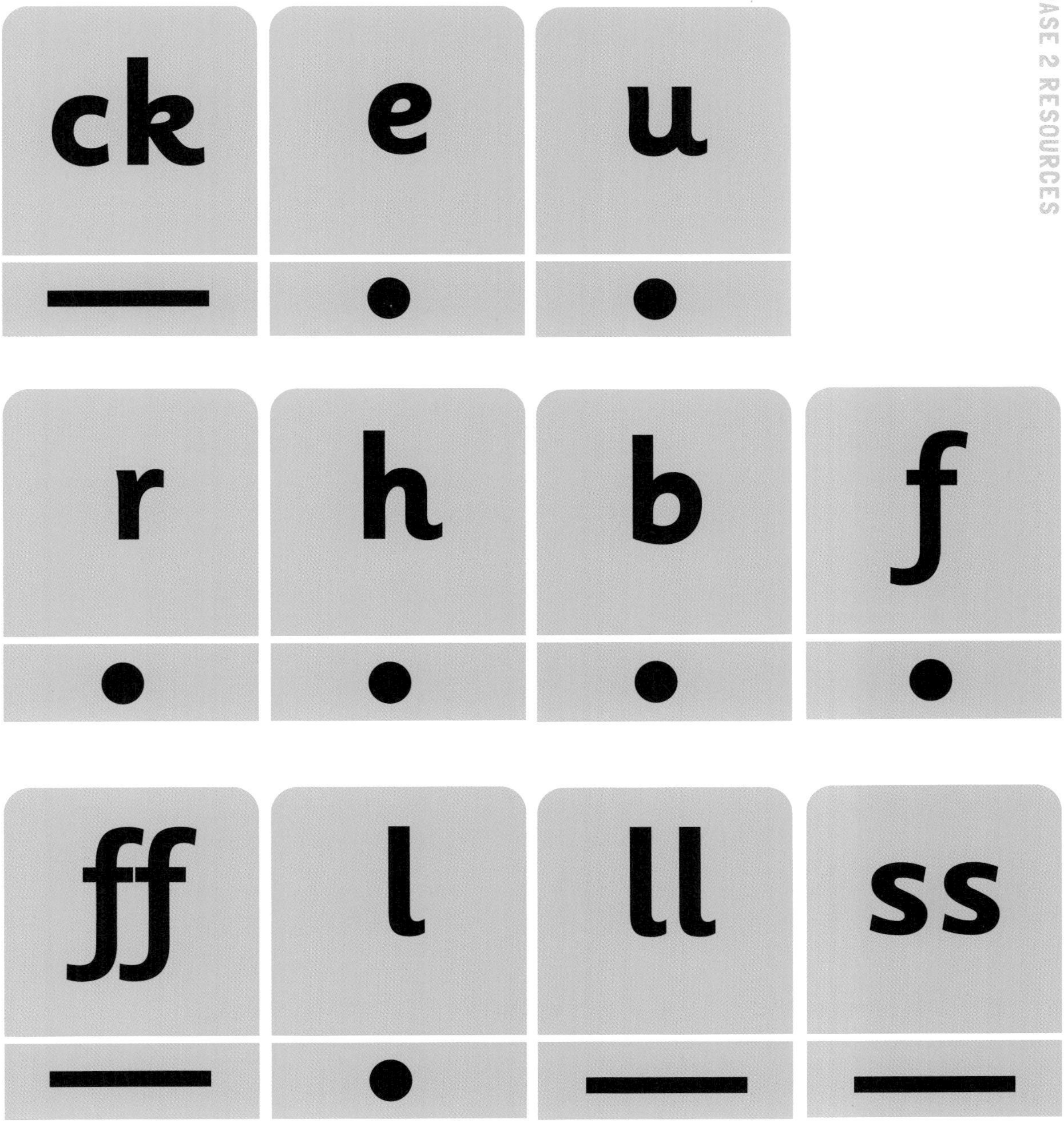

ck

e

u

r

h

b

f

ff

l

ll

ss

EXAMPLE FLASH CARDS

sat	pin	map
• • •	• • •	• • •
gas	dog	kick
• • •	• • •	• • —
cup	hop	bat
• • •	• • •	• • •
puff	bell	kiss
• • —	• • —	• • —

WORDS WITH PHASE 2 SOUNDS

Here are some words to practise reading, which include the Phase 2 sounds. Only start trying out words when your child is familiar with the Phase 2 sounds on pages 68–69. For the **HIGH FREQUENCY WORDS** taught during this phase, please go to page 124. Though they seem random, these words are given in the order in which most kids will learn them through phonics.

sat	can	hop
pat	cot	hat
tap	cap	hug
sit	cat	bad
set	kid	bag
pit	kit	bed
tip	kick	bug
pip	sock	bus
sip	sack	bun
pan	pick	bat
pin	sick	bit
tin	pack	fit
nap	get	fun
am	pet	fog
man	ten	puff
mat	net	huff
map	pen	fat
sad	peg	lap
dip	men	let
did	neck	leg
tag	run	lot
gap	mug	lit
gas	cup	bell
pig	sun	doll
dig	tuck	fill
got	mud	tell
on	rip	less
not	rat	hiss
pot	rag	mass
top	rug	fuss
dog	rot	miss
pop	hot	kiss

PHASE 3

Phase 3 in phonics introduces more letters and more sounds. It starts by covering the rest of the letters in the alphabet.

j	the **j** in **jump**
v	the **v** in **van**
w	the **w** in **wet**
x	the **x** in **box** – pronounced **/ks/**
y	the **y** in **yoghurt**
z, zz	the **z** in **buzz**
qu	the **qu** in **queen** – pronounced **/kw/** (children aren't taught the **q** on its own as a sound at this stage as it's rarely seen on its own in words)

After this, children are taught the following digraphs (two letters making one sound) and trigraphs (three letters making one sound). I have put example words next to them to help you out with the sounds they make, as on their own they can be confusing.

ai	the **ai** in **rain** – pronounced **/ay/**
ee	the **ee** in **feet**
igh	the **igh** in **light**
oa	the **oa** in **boat** – pronounced **/oh/**
oo	the **oo** in **book** – the short sound for **oo** is like **/uh/** (accent dependent)
oo	the **oo** in **food** – not a typo! These letters make a longer **/ooo/** sound.

ar	the **ar** in **card**
or	the **or** in **fork**
ur	the **ur** in **turn**
ow	the **ow** in **down**
oi	the **oi** in **coin** – pronounced **/oy/**
ear	the **ear** in **fear**
air	the **air** in **hair**
ure	the **ure** in **pure** – pronounced **/yooer/**
er	the **er** in **fern**
ch	the **ch** in **chop**
sh	the **sh** in **shell**
th	the **th** in **moth**
ng	the **ng** in **song**

When your child reaches this stage in phonics, they will be getting to know a lot of lovely little sounds that can make up hundreds of words, both real and nonsense ones. These sounds will be taught over many weeks, and are recapped throughout the first three years in school. Five-minute games are helpful to recognize these sounds because the more often we see them and play around with them, the better they will stick in your child's memory, and it's our memory that we rely on the most when learning to read.

In addition, this phase of phonics is usually when children will be really getting to grips with blending the sounds together to make words, so the games I've included over the next few pages are to practise **BLENDING** and **SEGMENTING** in five-minute bursts of fun at home!

By also playing games with words that make absolutely no sense, but that follow the rules of phonics, we can help our kids. Plus, sometimes the nonsense words that crop up in these games are great for a grown-up snigger. How frequently *nob*, *vag* and *cok* might appear can often be the decider for how much I want to play a game, because I am nothing if not a big kid.

If you don't have any sand, use porridge oats or dried rice or a tub of pasta. You could also use water beads – absolutely anything you like to bury the words!

SOME EXAMPLE WORDS FOR THIS GAME:

- **REAL TWO-LETTER WORDS:** it, in, up, at, on, an, am
- **NONSENSE TWO-LETTER WORDS:** ip, ut, na, mu, da, tu
- **REAL THREE-LETTER WORDS:** mop, pin, sat, pet, pen, get, run, sun, men, met, peg, cap, map, rag
- **NONSENSE THREE-LETTER WORDS:** rop, pum, nas, gud, mig, nos, lub, tod, fap, afs, upt
- **REAL FOUR-LETTER WORDS:** huff, kiss, sell, lock, tuck, pack, pain, week, wood, root, soap, town, join
- **NONSENSE FOUR-LETTER WORDS:** diff, woot, fush, poat, rull, poik, gure, vair, zoog, baim, wuck
- **REAL FIVE-LETTER WORDS:** beard, towel, tight, thing, shock, check, shell, boils, moths, flash
- **NONSENSE FIVE-LETTER WORDS:** clure, bighp, learg, voish, foips, daish, milue, fuper, beegs

BURIED TREASURE

This isn't a game of my invention, but it's one that I've played in every school I've taught in and have seen multiple times online. It's a classic when it comes to familiarizing kids with phonics sounds, blending and also recognizing whether the sounds make a real word or not. You can play this in a variety of different ways. It can be done simply with a box and paper. Or (if you want to drive all your colleagues barmy in a school) push together a few tables to make a 'pirate ship', let the kids sit on top of it, bury the words in a sandpit, and sing 'Yo ho, yo ho!' at the tops of your voices as you pretend to sail the seven seas. The kids in my class obviously loved that – I'm not sure the teachers in the neighbouring classrooms did quite as much!

GRAB:

- some yellow, gold or silver paper – foil is good too
- a pen
- a treasure box
- a sandpit or something you can put sand in

TO SET UP . . .

1. Cut the paper into circles to make coin shapes – this is your 'treasure'.
2. On each bit of treasure write a word: five real words and five made-up words.
3. Bury the treasure in the sand.

TO PLAY . . .

1. Let your child dig through the sand to find a piece of treasure.
2. They have to read it and decide if it is real treasure (a real word) or fake (a nonsense word).
3. If it is treasure, they pop it in their treasure box.
4. If it is fake, they can throw it away.

Keep their creations out for a few days and keep moving them around. Perhaps pop them in their bedroom to say out loud when they get dressed or in the bathroom to recap as they brush their teeth. Make a folder or a basket to keep them all in if they like, then they will have their own phonics book!

SOUND ART

Now, this isn't a game as such, but it's a couple of ideas for children who are more visual learners. I worked with a lot of children like this when I was a teaching assistant and this is an activity that I found to be very useful.

GRAB:

- masking tape
- newspaper
- paper
- any kind of paints, arts or crafts stuff you have

TO SET UP . . .

1. Use masking tape and newspaper to cover the table you're working at!

TO PLAY 1 . . .

1. Whatever sound you are focusing on, draw it in big bubble writing, as shown in the photo on the opposite page.
2. Say out loud a few words that have the sounds you want to cover.
3. Ask your child which word they like the best. It's important that they decide this for themselves.
4. Tell them to colour in or decorate the sounds you've drawn that way. So if the sound was **/ay/** and they like the word **rain**, then they could make the drawn **ai** look like clouds with raindrops coming out of them. Some examples of ones we made are opposite.

TO PLAY 2 . . .

1. Fold a strip of paper into three.
2. On the left-hand side write the letter or sound (grapheme) clearly.
3. As with the first game, say out loud a few words with the sound in.
4. In the middle of the paper, write the word your child chose, and on the right-hand side let them draw a picture to match. Now they have their own foldable flash card!

PUZZLE BLENDING

Ewan found blending so tricky; he just couldn't hear how the sounds could fit together to make words. I played these kinds of games with him many times before he started getting it, so don't worry if, the first twenty times you play, you are the only one modelling how to blend the sounds together, with very loooonnnggg clues to help them. They will get it eventually, and this game is perfect to support them as they do.

GRAB:

- a bit of cardboard (ideally from a cardboard box)
- a whiteboard pen
- a marker pen
- scissors
- dice
- sellotape or sticky-back plastic

TO SET UP . . .

1. Cut a strip off your piece of card and cut it into three connecting puzzle pieces.
2. Put sellotape or sticky-back plastic over each puzzle piece.
3. On the remainder of the card, or a bit of paper if there isn't enough card left, draw an outline of each puzzle piece across the top, then draw lines on either side of them so that each puzzle outline is at the top of a column.
4. Then write the numbers 1 to 6 down the left-hand side. Draw a long line under the numbers, crossing the lines of the puzzle columns, so you end up with a grid with three columns of boxes and six rows.
5. In each box of the grid, write a letter or letters (depending on which level of phonics your little one is up to).
6. The middle column must have vowels or vowel digraphs in it.

TO PLAY . . .

1. Your child selects one puzzle piece, then rolls the dice.
2. Identify which column in the grid has the puzzle piece that they've picked. Then, in that column, go down to the row number that matches the number on the dice they've just thrown.
3. They need to sound out the letter or letters that they land on and write the letter/sound on to the puzzle piece with the whiteboard pen.

4. Then pick another puzzle piece, roll the dice and write the letter/sound on the puzzle piece. We sometimes play as a three and each takes a turn to do one piece, or they play this solo.
5. Roll and write until you have a letter/sound on each of the puzzle pieces.
6. Now connect the pieces together and make the word. Is it a real word or a nonsense word? Can you make some really silly and funny words?
7. Wipe the letters off the puzzle pieces with your fingers and start again.

Obviously you can play with digraphs too; your kiddo would just have to catch two letters at once and place them into the same box. F-i-sh, for example, would go into the three boxes.

SEGMENT HOPPING

Segmenting is the opposite of blending. It is where your child is chopping a word up into its separate sounds. It is a useful skill to have, especially when it comes to them being able to spell words once they start writing them. So this game is designed to practise that in a physical way. I often find that when my two play a physical game, the giggles come thick and fast, which always means they want to play for longer. The win here is two-fold. They think they are getting away with a long game, and I know they are learning something. Plus, I can then flick the TV on with zero guilt afterwards!

GRAB:

- masking tape
- lots of letters in any form, such as magnetic letters or flash cards
- something to catch the letters in, like a box, bowl, bucket, saucepan or net

TO SET UP . . .

1. Select five words. Choose words with as many letters as your child is confident with. For example, if they are working on CVC words, choose five of those – such as *cat, mop, sit, pin* and *dip.*
2. Create a line of boxes out of masking tape on the floor. It needs to have as many boxes as your words have sounds, and each box needs to be big enough for your child to stand in.
3. Collect together the letters needed to create all the words you've selected. So, for this example, I'd grab **c, a, t, m, o, p, s, i, t, n** and **d.**

TO PLAY . . .

1. Your child stands to one side of the masking-tape grid holding the bowl, or whatever you're using for them to catch with.
2. You tell them a word. They then have to try to segment that word into sounds. When they think they have the first sound, they hop into the first box on the floor. They say the sound or keep guessing until they say the correct sound.
3. You then throw them the letter (or letters) that make that sound, and they have to try to catch it in the bowl!
4. If they catch it, they can pop it in the box they are standing in, then step into the next one and say the next sound of the word.
5. If they miss it, throw the letter (or letters) around again until they catch them. Keep going until they've made the whole word.

VARIATIONS

- Select by dipping in a large spoon and flicking a bit of paper into the air.
- Select by using a straw and sucking hard on the paper to lift it out of the bowl.
- Put your hands behind your back and get out the letters with your teeth only.
- Take off a sock and use your toes to get out the letters.
- Screw the letters into tiny balls and fire them out of a straw like a pea-shooter.
- Pop paper clips on to each letter and use a magnet to select them.
- Tip all the letters over your kiddo's head and see which ones they catch.

EXTRA SILLY SOUP

Silly Soup is a game from *Give Me Five* that is excellent for practising blending sounds together into words. It's a game I learned when working in schools and we've played it many times at home. But we don't always play it the same way. We make it sillier and sillier each time, because where's the fun in doing the same thing over and over again? But don't worry if you haven't got *Give Me Five*, because here it is with some additional ways in which we add some extra silly seasoning!

GRAB:

- 2 bits of paper or card in different colours
- pen
- scissors
- large bowl or container
- wooden spoon
- additional things to grab, depending on which version you are playing: straws, paper clips

TO SET UP . . .

1. Write consonants or consonant digraphs (**sh**, **ch**, **th**, **ng**) on one colour of paper, then cut them out individually.
2. Write vowels or vowel digraphs/trigraphs (**oa**, **ai**, **igh**) on the other colour, then cut them out individually.
3. Fold up all the bits of paper with letters on and pop them in a large bowl.

TO PLAY . . .

1. Ask your child to select two bits of paper of the consonant colour and one of the vowel. Here's where the silliness comes in! See the variations opposite for silly ways to select the letters.
2. Once you've selected your three bits of paper in whatever silly way you like, open up the bits of paper to reveal what word you have created. Don't forget to swap the letters around in different ways, so if you've got **m**, **o** and **p**, you can read them as both **mop** and **pom**.

PHASE 3 RESOURCES

Here are the sounds set out for you to use as flash cards for games or as a reference point.

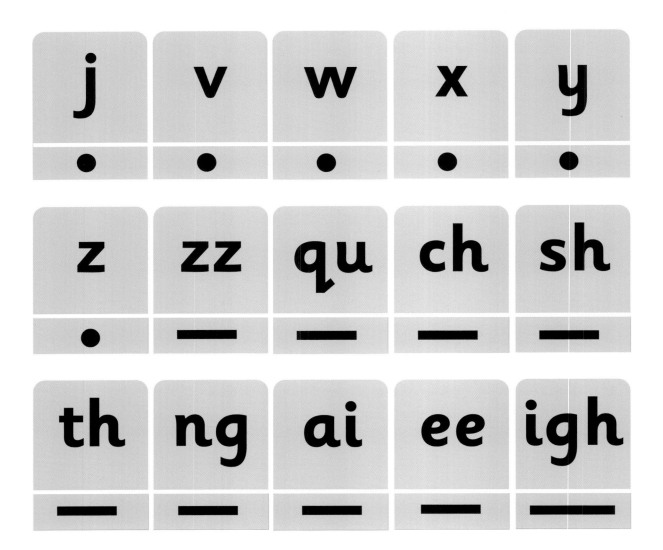

The dots and dashes under the letters are sound buttons (see page 42 for an explanation), and on page 86 I've also given you an example of how you could create your own flash cards.

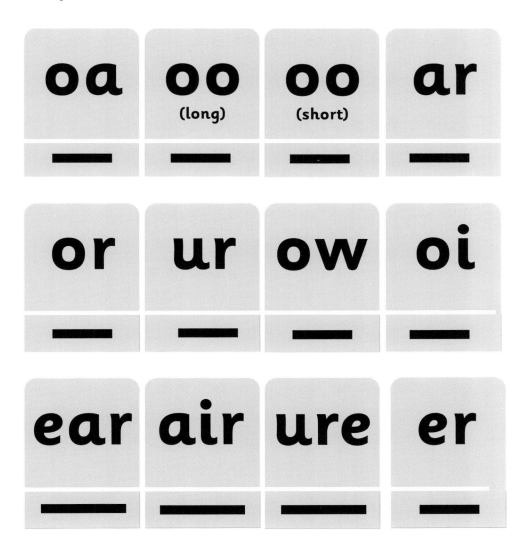

oa | oo (long) | oo (short) | ar

or | ur | ow | oi

ear | air | ure | er

EXAMPLE FLASH CARDS

jam • • •	vet • • •	zip • • •
quack — • —	chip — • •	ship — • •
song • • —	boot • — •	town • — •
fair • — •	sheet — — •	march • — —

WORDS WITH PHASE 3 SOUNDS

For the **HIGH FREQUENCY WORDS** taught during this phase, please go to page 124.

jam	song	join
jet	rain	hear
van	tail	near
vet	feet	hair
win	deep	fair
web	light	sure
mix	high	manure
box	coat	ladder
yes	road	dinner
yell	zoo	tooth
zip	boot	torch
buzz	foot	sheet
quick	took	chain
quack	car	farmer
chin	bark	church
chip	fork	sheep
shop	fort	march
ship	turn	longer
bash	burp	shook
moth	cow	powder
thin	town	
rang	coin	

PHASE 4

Now Phase 4 is a weird one. When children reach this phase, they don't learn any new sounds. This phase is often taught at around ages five and six. It's really a recap period for the children to take all the sounds they have learned in Phases 2 and 3 and to practise using them in different ways to make longer and more complicated words.

The main thing they will be doing is playing about with words that contain different combinations of consonant sounds. As they work through this phase, the words they're learning to read will get more complex – combining digraphs and trigraphs they've already learned, alongside groups of single consonant sounds that are often tricky to pick out individually in speech. For example: the **nd** together in the word **pond** or the **st** together in the word **stand**. And finally they'll move on to three consonants together like the **scr** in **scrunch**. These groups of letters aren't digraphs and trigraphs, they are common consonant combinations.

Here are some of the consonant/vowel word patterns (with examples) that children might be learning and practising to read and write:

C stands for a consonant or consonant digraph, like **sh** or **ng**.

V stands for a vowel or vowel digraph, like **ee** or **ai**.

CVCC   words with two consonants together at the end, like **help** or **went**

CCVC   words with two consonants together at the start, like **green** or **train**

CCVCC   words with two consonants together at the start and the end, like **stand** or **crisp**

CCCVC   words where three consonants occur together at the start, like **strap** or **scrap**

CCCVCC   words with consonant combinations at the start and end, like **sprint** and **string**

Now, I just want to remind you that as parents you do not need to memorize the Cs and Vs and their various combinations. **ALL** you need to know here is that children are learning longer words (or polysyllabic words, which just means more than one syllable). They're being asked to sound out more letters at once and to practise blending them together. This is the stage where reading with them will help more than ever, but if you want some examples of words to play with during this phase, then turn to pages 96 and 97.

Below are some examples of the kind of words your children will be practising at this stage:

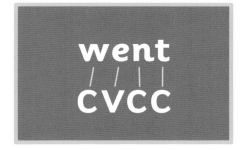

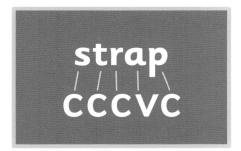

See how digraphs like **ch** are treated as one consonant sound, and in the same way **ee** is one vowel sound.

Children also learn more **HIGH FREQUENCY WORDS** in Phase 4, which you can find on page 125.

YES/NO ESCAPE ROOM

The Yes/No game is an easy game you can play for this phase with your little ones. It's suggested in the government's *Letters and Sounds* document so lots of kids will be familiar with this from school. In traditional **FIVE MINUTE MUM** style, I've amended this commonly played classroom game to make it a bit more physical and exciting, because often kids have a lot of energy even after a full day at school. I find it's best to wear them out so I can sit on the sofa with a chocolate orange come 7 p.m.!

GRAB:

- paper or Post-it notes
- pen
- masking tape
- timer – for example, a sand timer, stopwatch or smartphone

TO SET UP . . .

1. Write five to ten questions clearly on paper or Post-its that use the words your child is practising – simple questions your child can answer yes or no to.

   Here are some examples from *Letters and Sounds*:

   Can a clock get cross?
   Can crabs clap hands?
   Did a shark ever jump over a tree?
   Is the moon green?
   Have you ever slept in a tent?
   Are you afraid of thunderstorms?
   Do chimps come from mars?
   Do trains run on tracks?

2. Cut each question out separately if using paper and stick them all around a room in your house, high up and down low.
3. Write **LOCK** on a strip of masking tape and have it ready to stick across the door, as shown in the photo opposite.

TO PLAY . . .

1. Go with your child into the room where the clues are and tape the door shut with the masking tape that says **LOCK**.
2. Explain to your child that there are questions around the room. They must answer them all correctly to escape and they have however long you wish to set to get out! (We usually do thirty seconds per question.)
3. Give them a pen so they can write their answer to each question. They can do them in any order – the aim is to just answer them all.
4. Say '**GO!**' and start the timer.
5. At the end, once they've answered all the questions, they must tell you how many have the answer **YES** and how many have the answer **NO** before they're allowed to rip off the tape and escape.

Sometimes I randomly put questions like this around the house with a Post-it on a door, and in order for the kids to pass through it they have to read and answer YES or NO.

Some children panic when a timer is involved and it can put them off. So just take the timer away and do it with them if this is the case.

If you're kiddos need motivation, tell them all the words are the password for having the TV back on!

ICY WORDS

From a very young age, my two enjoyed playing with ice. We'd drop ice cubes in a water tray (just an old plastic box) and I'd give them a big spoon to fish them out and watch them disappear like magic. Then when Ewan and Florence got a bit bigger, I used to put toys into cups of water and freeze them so they could smash them out with a wooden spoon. But what to do now they are older? Is ice play over? Not quite. I still set up ice play when I'm freezing myself some cubes for a G&T on a hot day . . .

GRAB:

- some paper or plastic cups
- plastic letters
- spoons or toy hammer
- jug of warm water
- tray

TO SET UP . . .

1. Put the letters into words. It totally depends on your child's capability which words you choose.
2. Drop each word into a cup and fill it with water.
3. Keep them in the freezer for a few hours.
4. Have the tray with the water jug and spoons ready.

TO PLAY . . .

1. Pop the ice out of the cups on to the tray.
2. Tell your child they have to smash or melt the ice to get the letters out.
3. Once they have got all the letters out from one cup, encourage them to rearrange them into a word. Can they guess what the word is? Help with clues if needed.

FIVE QUICK IDEAS FOR PHASE 4

For all these speedy games use the words on the resources pages 96–97 to guide you.

1. SILENT SIMON SAYS

Play **SIMON SAYS** but after you say '*Simon says*', instead of saying the instruction out loud, hold up a bit of paper with a word on. The instruction could be . . .

- sit
- stand
- spin
- run
- jump
- hop
- melt
- nod
- star jump
- clap
- twist
- stamp

Write these down on pieces of paper before you begin and get playing!

2. CHOP, CHOP

Write out some words from this phase on craft foam or card. Get out some scissors and encourage your child to cut up the words. Can they find the digraphs and cut them out, or can they chop them into the bits they can sound out? Keep chopping in as many ways they like. Now mix up the chopped bits of the different words and see what funny nonsense words you can make. If you're using craft foam, you can stick your words to windows using water!

3. PUZZLE BLENDING EXTENSION

Play the **PUZZLE BLENDING** game from page 78. But this time, instead of writing single letters on the puzzle pieces, write digraphs. Put digraphs with vowels in the middle column and some common consonant combinations (like **st**, **br**, **gr**) or digraphs in the left column and single letters in the right-hand column. What real and nonsense words can you come up with?

4. CORRECTION

Write out a few sentences with mistakes in. For example: 'The milk is blue' or 'My hair is a nest' (keep the sentences short and words simple). Give your child a different-coloured pen to 'mark' your work and let them tell you where you've gone wrong. They can cross out the mistakes and write the correct answers in if they like. If they aren't keen to write, ask them how to spell it and you write the correction.

5. TODDLER PONG

A classic game from my website is perfect for this phase! Write words/letters/digraphs for this phase on bits of paper and fold them up, then get some cups and a bouncy ball. Pop one bit of paper in each cup. Your child has to bounce the ball and, when it lands in a cup, they get to open the paper in the cup and read the word, letter or digraph. Keep playing until they've managed to bounce the ball into every cup.

PHASE 4 RESOURCES

There are no new sounds to learn in this phase. At this stage, they're learning to blend different consonant sounds as they learn more difficult words. Here are some example words to help them to practise this.

CVCC WORDS

These words help children to practise words with two consonant sounds together at the end or middle of a word.

tent	hand	paint
band	milk	think
lamp	jump	sandpit
nest	chest	handstand
sink	bench	milking
soft	thank	shampoo
bank	shelf	thunder

CCVC WORDS

These words help children to practise words with two consonant sounds together at the beginning of a word.

stop	green	brown
frog	trees	spark
step	smell	spoon
track	train	brush
glad	start	scoop
twin	clown	treetop
clap	star	floating

CCVCC, CCCVC AND CCCVCC WORDS

These words help children to practise more complex words with more blended consonant sounds in them.

stand	slept	scrap
spend	crunch	street
twist	shrink	scratch
brand	printer	sprint
stamp	string	strand

For the **HIGH FREQUENCY WORDS** taught during this phase, go to page 125.

Please remember that you don't need to memorize these patterns for consonant and vowel sounds! These are just example words that you can use to play Phase 4 games.

PHASE 5

This phase is typically taught in a child's second year at school. As you will see, teachers work through the phonics phases slowly, doing lots of recapping of sounds and practising different ways to use them. If you are doing the same at home, then you're doing a fantastic job. Even going back over Phase 3 sounds with confident readers is never a bad idea. Playing something they find super easy will continue to build their confidence and increase their enjoyment, so never feel it's a wasted game if they fly through it.

The new sounds that our kids will be introduced to in Phase 5 are:

ay	– day	aw	– saw
ou	– out	wh	– when
ie	– tie	ph	– phone
ea	– eat	ew	– new
oy	– boy	oe	– toe
ir	– girl	au	– haul
ue	– blue	ey	– monkey

Then we come to the split digraphs. These are where two letters make a particular sound, but they are split up by another letter.

GO BACK TO BASICS

When your child is first learning these new Phase 5 sounds, don't forget to still play all the games from the previous phases where recognition is the aim. These games are marked with this star to help you find them.

This just means they can be played with anything they are learning. So make up a new set of flash cards and let the games commence!

ALTERNATIVES

In this phase, our children will also start to be taught some alternative sounds that familiar letters can make.

So, even though they know the letter **i** makes an **/ih/** sound, they will be taught that in some words that letter makes an **/eye/** sound. For example, **bin = /ih/** and **find = /eye/**. The same letter, on its own, making two different sounds. Some single words can have a double pronunciation – think of **wind**. Did you read it as in 'wind the bobbin up'? Or as in 'there's a strong wind today'?

Children are taught these alternatives so that when they come across a word in reading that has a letter (or letters) that has multiple sounds, they can try saying it with the alternatives to hear which one makes sense. So if they were to read this sentence:

The bird ate some bread.

They might get stuck on the word **bread** as they have previously been told that the **ea** makes an **/ee/** sound in words. So they would sound out: **b-r-ee-d**. But, if they know that the **ea** can also make an **/eh/** sound, they would try the alternative sound and know that **b-r-eh-d** makes much more sense.

The following is a guide to the alternative sounds that letters make, but I'm mindful that some sounds may be different depending on your accent. Don't worry about this – there's no need to teach your child the Queen's English! Say the sounds and words as you would normally, and explain any difference between them as simply as you can. There are always going to be slight differences in the way we all pronounce words.

i	– win, find
o	– sock, old
c	– cat, ceiling
g	– gown, giant
u	– but, put (accent dependent)
a	– mat, what
y	– yes, fly, berry
ow	– cow, glow
ie	– pie, field
ea	– meat, bread
er	– otter, her
ch	– chin, school, chef
ou	– out, shoulder, could, you

Now, you DO NOT need to memorize these or even really need to know them at all. You just need to know what to say to support your child when they come across these alternatives – and it's simply this: 'Oh, yes – that's another way to say/spell that sound.' A basic acknowledgement can go a really long way with kids. Also highlight that they aren't 'wrong' with what they said, as in some words that is exactly the sound they might need. This simple act of validation and understanding is often massively helpful when it comes to supporting your child's reading. As always, it's playing games that will help secure these variations in their memories.

TOP TIP: Something I used to do when helping kids who were learning to write during this phase of phonics was to give them options. For example, a child might try to write the word **great** and will sound out the **g-r** and then get stuck. I'd write **ai** and **ea** and **ay** down on a separate piece of paper and explain that all those letter combinations make the sound they're looking for, and let them select which they think it is by circling the options. I would then tell them when they get the correct one for their word. This next game expands on that idea in a more fun way!

This is a good game if your child confuses two letters like b and d. You could shout words with the sounds in, such as dog, mad, muddy and bog, about and grab. Can they hear the b or d sound and recognize the correct letter to match?

You could also play this with two buckets and lots of screwed-up newspaper or balls. Each bucket has a different sound stuck on the front and they have to throw the balls into the correct bucket for each word!

WHICH IS IT?

This is a game that my lovely friend Gina came up with. Gina's children, Joe and Emily, are a few years older than mine, but she enjoys playing five-minute games with them so always finds ways to adapt games to suit those a few years ahead. What always amazes me is how a simple game you might think your child would find 'babyish' can easily be made fun for older ones by upping the ante. Add in a timer, or make it competitive, and suddenly it isn't for babies any more – it's '*I want to beat you!*'

GRAB:

- ■ paper
- ■ pen

TO SET UP . . .

1. Write down ten words that have the same sound but are represented in two different ways. For example, the **/j/** sound can be made by **j** or **g**. Example words could be: *jump, just, joke, join, jelly*; and *giant, gentle, gem, magic, ginger*.
2. Write a big J on one bit of paper and stick it to one end of a room, and a big G on the other and stick that at the opposite side of the room. (Feel free to mix it up by using capitals instead of lower-case letters, since kids need to learn both.)

TO PLAY . . .

1. You shout out one word at a time.
2. Your child listens to the word and runs to the letter they think makes the sound in the word.
3. They bash the letter with their hand and run back to you for the next word.
4. Time them if they like, or keep score of how many they get right. Play again and see if they can beat it!

VARIATIONS

Here are some good alternative sounds and words to play this with:

/s/ sound	s: sand, sort, sit, last, silly
	c: ceiling, cycle, central, acid, cell
/k/ sound	c: can, cup, scan, cat, cold
	ch: Christmas, school, chord, echo, anchor
/oh/ sound	ow: snow, grow, show, low, mow
	oa: boat, coat, moat, goat, float

VARIATIONS

■ Roll a train on a train track with letters written on Post-it notes underneath.

■ Push a toy car along a paper or cardboard track with words/sounds written on.

■ Put some sellotape over a strip of cardboard to make a slide for a favourite soft toy. Write the word on the slide and say the sounds as the toy slides down.

■ Write the sounds on separate bits of paper and let your child scoot, jump or hop along them as they say them.

■ Put any form of sounds/letters on top of some cushions. Let your child drag the cushions towards each other as they blend each sound together.

Use whatever your child likes best to support this activity – a favourite toy, doll, things to do. Go with their interests and you'll find they are more willing.

ROLL OVER

When it comes to blending sounds together, I find some children prefer to do this while moving their bodies. An occupational therapist once wrote a guest blog for me on my website about why children fidget, and how helpful it can be for them to physically move while they are trying to compute something in their head. It's useful to remember this when kids read books, as sometimes they like to wriggle around. It can be really quite annoying for an adult, with a kid squirming next to you as you try to read a story, but they can't help it! So if you too have a little one with ants in their pants, perhaps these ideas might help . . .

GRAB:

- chalk
- pen
- paper
- letters of any kind
- any kind of toy or vehicle on wheels – skateboard, bike, scooter, roller-skates, toy vehicle and so on

TO SET UP . . .

1. On pieces of paper, write words for your kiddo to read but separate out the letters into their sounds, with spaces between each sound.
So **c a t** or **ch ur ch**.

TO PLAY . . .

1. Let your child roll their vehicle over each sound.
2. Encourage them to say the sound out loud.
3. Ask them to move their vehicle and say the sounds again, and repeat a few times.
4. Encourage them to go faster or say the sounds slower and longer, and see if they can blend the sounds together and hear the word they're making.

ay ou ie ea oy

ir ue aw wh ph

ew oe au ey

SOME EXAMPLE WORDS WITH THESE DIGRAPHS:

play	out	lie
meat	toy	girl
blue	saw	when
phone	new	toe
autumn	they	make
like	bone	rule

SPLIT DIGRAPHS

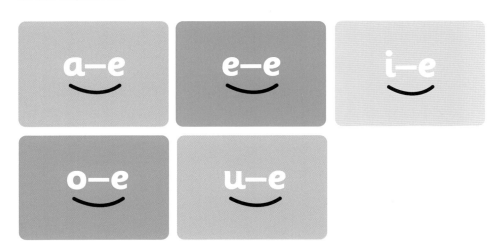

a-e   e-e   i-e

o-e   u-e

LETTERS AND SOUNDS

The following grids list some of the alternatives for written letters (graphemes) and the sounds they make, and I've given examples of words to help make it clearer. The first grid below shows the alternative sounds children will be taught during this phase.

WRITTEN LETTER	SOUND YOU HEAR	EXAMPLE WORD
i	/ih/ /eye/	ink find
o	/o/ /oh/	on both
c	/c/ /sss/	cat ceiling
g	/g/ /j/	go giant
u	/u/ /yoo/	up human
ow	/ow/ /oh/	cow blow
ie	/eye/ /ee/	pie field
ea	/ee/ /eh/	bead bread
er	/ah/ /er/	letter (accent dependent) fern
a	/a/ /o/	apple what
y	/y/ /ee/	yoghurt very
ch	/ch/ /sh/	chip chef
ou	/ow/ /u/	out could

SOUND YOU HEAR	WRITTEN LETTER	EXAMPLE WORD
/c/	c k ck qu x ch	cat kite duck mosquito excited school
/ch/	ch tch	chip match
/f/	f ph	fun phone
/j/	j g dge	jump giant bridge
/m/	m mb	mat climb
/n/	n kn gn	nan knee gnome
/r/	r wr	run write
/s/	s c sc	sun ceiling scent
/sh/	sh ch ti s ss c	shark charlotte reception tension mission special
/v/	v ve	van live
/w/	w wh	wind white
/e/	e ea	egg bread

This grid (which continues on pages 110–111) shows some of the most commonly found alternative letters for particular sounds grouped together. There are always exceptions, of course, because English is very complex, but I hope these lists might be useful to refer to when supporting your child at home with their reading and writing at this stage of learning.

SOUND YOU HEAR	WRITTEN LETTER	EXAMPLE WORD
/ee/	e ee y ey ea e-e ie	be feet happy donkey sea these shield
/o/	o a	on what
/u/	oo u oul o	look put should son
/ai/	ai ay a-e eigh ey ei	rain play make eight grey rein
/igh/	igh y ie i-e	light fly pie like
/oa/	oa ow oe o-e o	boat grow toe bone go
/oo/	oo ew ue ou	poo grew blue you
/yoo/	ue u-e ew	rescue cube few
/ar/	ar a	car fast (accent dependent)

SOUND YOU HEAR	WRITTEN LETTER	EXAMPLE WORD
/or/	or aw au al our	fork awful cause walk pour
/ur/	ur ir er ear our	turn girl serve heard colour
/ow/	ow ou	cow ground
/oi/	oi oy	coin boy
/ear/	ear ere eer	fear here deer

For the **HIGH FREQUENCY WORDS** taught during this phase, go to page 125.

PHASE 6

By the time your child reaches Phase 6 they are likely to be reading more fluently, so we are now getting into the nitty gritty of the English language. Funny rules, alternatives and a bit of grammar too. This phase is often taught in your child's third year at school and is the final part of phonics. However, the things they have learned during the previous phases will continue to support them throughout their time in primary school as they master fluent reading and confident writing.

A big focus in this phase is **SUFFIXES**. Suffixes are letters that go at the end of words to change their meaning. So, you add an **s** to make something plural or add **ing** to indicate tense. It is at this point, if you're reading how phonics is taught in the government's *Letters and Sounds* document, that your head starts to hurt if you aren't a teacher. I include myself in this.

For example, children need to know and understand, for the following words, that when adding a suffix to them, the **y** at the end of the original word might need to change into an **i**. But not always . . . !

- **employ(ment)** – no change needed
- **merry(ment)** – yes, merriment
- **play(ed)** – no
- **silly(ness)** – yes, silliness

FFS! It's a wonder that any of us can read or write at all, isn't it? Aren't our brains magnificent for knowing stuff like this?!

Some examples of suffixes that children are taught in Phase 6:

-ing (drink ing)   -y (sand y)

-ed (dust ed)   -s (run s)

-er (fast er)   -es (bush es)

-est (slow est)   -ment (pay ment)

-ful (care ful)   -ness (dark ness)

-ly (bright ly)

Unfortunately, English doesn't do simple, and you can't just bung a suffix on the end of all words and they will make sense. Sometimes the original word needs to change a teeny bit when you add the suffix, in order to spell it correctly. For example, if you want to add **ing** to the end of the word **smile** you need to remove the **e**. There are lots of little rules around these that children will be shown at school. Here are some:

- Adding -**s** or -**es** in words like **park**, **dish**

- Removing the **e** before adding -**ing** on words like **ride**, **bake**, **hike**, **wave**

- Changing a **y** to an **i** before adding -**ed** or -**er** or -**es** in words like **lucky**, **worry**, **funny**, **copy**, **puppy**

- Adding an extra consonant to words like **stop** – **stopPing**, **nod** – **nodDing**, **skip** – **skipPed**

DO I REALLY KNOW THIS?

This phase of phonics can go through some very specific rules in the language that can help to support the understanding of these changes, but let me tell you something: I do not know those rules, and perhaps you might not either – yet here you are reading this book and here I am writing it.

The thing about this stage of phonics is that the best thing we can do to support our children swings right back to the beginning of this chapter and what it is all about: reading books together. Writing also starts to become more important at this age, the games for which you can find in the next chapter of this book. Those are the games I would recommend for when your child gets to this stage of phonics: games for spellings. Because no doubt this is where the crossover will occur. As your child starts learning about suffixes, the teachers will probably send home spellings to learn, which practise adding suffixes. So it's time to start mixing in spelling games, which can be found on page 165–187, alongside phonics games.

A band of pipers was playing.
"They are playing bagpipes." said
Chip.

"What a fantastic sound." said Biff.
"And they are wearing kilts."

6   7

Kipper drew a picture
of the mountains.

Biff took a photo

"Let's go and watch them,"
said Dad. "It will be fun.."

A band of
playing.

...land Games.'

If your child is reluctant to read a book brought home from school, be sneaky and use that to create your sentences!

PASS THE STORY

This is a game based on **PASS THE PARCEL**. Kids love that game, and, believe it or not, it isn't just the thought of a sweet or prize at the end that makes them love it. The joy of opening a parcel, it seems, is enough to hold their attention. I've received many a surprised message from fellow parents who have played this game with their child, expecting a full meltdown about the lack of prize, only to find they all enjoyed themselves. So if you want to add a wee treat into it, by all means do, but know that just playing with you is always enough . . .

GRAB:

- pen
- paper
- newspaper
- masking tape (or any tape will do)
- something to play music on

TO SET UP . . .

1. Write down a story of five to ten sentences.
2. If you don't want to make one up, summarize a book they love.
3. Cut out the sentences individually and mix up the order.
4. Wrap a sentence up like a parcel using the newspaper and tape.
5. Wrap the first parcel again, concealing a second sentence inside, and continue this way, building layers of the parcel, each with a sentence inside.
6. Get the music ready, so you can start it as soon as you play the game.

TO PLAY . . .

1. Sit down with your child. If there are a few of you, sit in a circle. Start the music.
2. Pass the parcel around the circle and, when the music stops, the person holding the parcel opens one layer. They read the sentence.
3. Continue playing until all the layers have been unwrapped.
4. Now see if you can figure out the story by putting the sentences in the correct order.

FIVE QUICK IDEAS FOR PHASE 6

Below are some ideas for speedy activities to support learning around this, including ones for suffixes and alternative spellings. If you do just one word or idea for five minutes in a day, that will build up gradually into LOADS of home support, which will help your children's confidence grow and grow. It doesn't always have to be a game. It can just be one quick interaction of some kind.

1. WRITER'S BLOCKS

For words that have apostrophes in, use connecting bricks to create the words and explain the spellings. So, for example, on the side of one long large brick write **they'll**, then on two smaller bricks (that together are the same size as the one with **they'll** written on), write **they** and **will** on the side. Then connect the smaller bricks on top or below the long brick to show your little ones how the apostrophes work. You could use words like these:

- they're – they / are
- I'll – I / will
- you've – you / have
- could've – could / have
- we're – we / are
- doesn't – does / not
- it's – it / is
- you're – you / are

2. SECRET CODES

On a piece of paper write the letters of the alphabet. Then next to **A** write **26**, then **25** next to **B** and so on until each letter has a number. Now write a note to your child on another bit of paper using the number code. So 'What would you like for lunch?' would be:

4,19,26,7   4,12,6,15,23   2,12,6   15,18,16,22   21,12,9   15,6,13,24,19?

Give them the code-cracking piece of paper and the message and see if they want to write you a secret message back.

3. LIFT THE FLAP

On the left-hand side of a piece of paper write two sets of words that can be shortened with apostrophes. So you could write **they will** and underneath write **does not**. Fold over the paper from the right-hand edge, so the paper covers the second word of each set and you can only see the first word. Now write the apostrophe abbreviation for each word on the folded-over paper (in this case: **'ll** and **'nt**) and cut a line under each. This should create a liftable flap so you can see the word that the apostrophe is shortening.

4. CHOOSE A RULE

Use magnetic letters on a metal baking tray or a radiator to write out a base word like **happy** and ask them to turn it into **happiness**. First discuss which of the rules they think it is: 1) change the **y**; 2) remove the **e**; or 3) add another letter. Once they've decided the rule, you give them the magnetic letters to reflect their choice, then let them put the word together and tell you if they think it's correct or not. If it isn't, ask them to select another rule.

5. SUFFIX OF THE DAY

Pop lots of bits of paper with different suffixes on (examples on page 118) into a box. Ask your child to select one each day, and you both have to try and think of a word that has that suffix. Write them down on a sheet of paper or whiteboard together. Perhaps make it a daily race to think of one and write it – you might even think of the same word! One a day makes learning suffixes much more manageable.

MNEMONICS

A mnemonic whereby the first letter of the word in a silly sentence is used as a way of remembering something – in this case how to spell difficult words. If your child is struggling to spell a particular word, see if you can come up with one together to help.

Because	– **Big Elephants Can Always Understand Small Elephants**
People	– **People Eat Orange Peel Like Elephants**
Friend	– **Friendly Raspberries In Every Nice Doughnut**
Little	– **Lie In Tiny Tents Like Eddie**

You can use sounds as well as letters! Ewan always remembers how to spell the vowel sound in **would**, **should** and **could** by saying '**OH, YOU LUCKY DUCK!**'

COMMON SUFFIXES

s	– **stop**s
es	– **crash**es
ed	– **park**ed
ing	– **send**ing
ful	– **use**ful
er	– **loud**er
est	– **dark**est
ly	– **bad**ly
ment	– **enjoy**ment
ness	– **sad**ness
y	– **milk**y

In these examples, none of the base words need to be changed. The suffix is added as it is, so you can play games matching the right suffix to the correct base word.

The next lists of words are examples where all the base words need to be changed before the suffix is added.

Words where you need to remove the *e*

like ➡ lik**ing**

fine ➡ fin**est**

bake ➡ bak**ed**

ride ➡ rid**er**

wave ➡ wav**ed**

Words where you need to change the **y** to **i**

marry ➡ marr**ied**

pony ➡ pon**ies**

lucky ➡ luck**ier**

hurry ➡ hurr**ied**

funny ➡ funn**ier**

Words where you need to add an extra one of the word's final **letter**

nod ➡ nod**ded**

run ➡ run**ning**

mad ➡ mad**der**

hop ➡ hop**per**

skip ➡ skip**ped**

HIGH FREQUENCY WORDS

(INCLUDING TRICKY WORDS, COMMON EXCEPTION WORDS, SIGHT WORDS OR WHATEVER YOU MIGHT CALL THEM!)

So, there is something I haven't covered yet when it comes to reading, isn't there? We've talked about books and gone through ALL of phonics, but there are lots of words in English that don't follow the rules of phonics. What about those? Children are taught these alongside phonics. The phonics phases include high frequency words (words that we use a lot in everyday life) to learn at each phase.

These are split into two types:

1. **DECODABLE** – which means we can use our phonics knowledge to sound them out.

2. **NON-DECODABLE** – which means we can't use our phonics knowledge; we just have to memorize them.

I have listed the main words in their various phases on pages 124–125. We don't need to focus too much on the decodable words as, once phonics gets going, children can figure those out. But, for the rest of them, there is no decoding or trick. It is simply about learning them by heart and for that there is only one thing to do – PLAY!

In this book, there are a few games you can play with these words to familiarize your children with them and you can adapt any of the recognition games with the star symbol:

- **OLD FIVE-MINUTE GAMES REVISITED – PAGE 67**

- **FLASH CARD MATCH-UP – PAGE 55**

- **SOUND SNAP (JUST CHANGE IT TO WORD SNAP!) – PAGE 61**

- **PASS THE STORY – PAGE 115**

- **FIVE QUICK IDEAS FOR PHASE 4 – PAGES 94–95**

These non-decodable words can also be known as:

- tricky words
- common exception words
- red words
- sight words
- dolch words

and I'm sure there are many more!

THEIR, THERE OR THEY'RE?

Now there are PLENTY of adults I know who still cannot get to grips with this. You might believe that in the age of social media and computers that this stuff isn't relevant, but try telling that to someone who has written the incorrect 'there' on their Facebook post got twenty-five comments telling them as much. This stuff still matters!

So how can we teach this to our kids in a nice easy way (and perhaps ourselves too!)?

It's common to confuse the three different spellings, especially **their** and **there**. Here are some basic definitions of what they all mean:

- **There** refers to a location, like **here** and **there**. (A good way to remember this one is that **there** contains **here**.) For example: **The horse is over there**.

- **Their** means it belongs to them. For example: **This is their book**.

- **They're** is a shorter way of saying **They are** – we use an apostrophe in place of the missing **a**. (If you're not sure about which spelling to use, try saying 'they are' in your sentence and if it still makes sense then the correct spelling is **they're**.) For example: **They're hungry**.

As much as I try to memorize all that, I still find imagery to be the most useful way to remember these spellings. This one is my favourite, which I've seen in lots of different versions on the internet (though no one seems to know the genius who thought of it):

And I've got the perfect game to help learn this . . .

their
there
they are

121

CATCH UP

This game was totally inspired by the TV quiz show *The Chase*. I love *The Chase*, and I've even got the kids into it too. There is nothing more fun than taking a game I love myself and turning it into something that kids will enjoy that will also teach them something. So here's what I did.

GRAB:

- cardboard
- pen
- paper
- scissors
- stopwatch
- a toy figure to represent each player (the tat box is an ideal source!)

TO SET UP . . .

1. Draw a seven-step board for your figures to hop along on the cardboard (as shown in the photo opposite).
2. Write six sentences on your paper: two with **their**, two with **there**, two with **they're** (there are some to get you started on the previous page).
3. Cut out three rectangles (buttons) for each player from the cardboard. One has **there** written on it, one has **their** written on it and the final one has **they're** written on it. If you like, you can add picture prompts for each too, as per the imagery on the previous page or like in the photo opposite.

TO PLAY . . .

1. Sit with your child so that you both have your three buttons in front of you. Both of your playing figures start on 1.
2. Ask your child if they want to select a level to start at. You can pretend there's money (for example, £100, £500 or £1,000) up for grabs as per the TV gameshow; or you can just say *beginner*, *learner* or *pro*.
3. If they select *beginner/£100* move their figure three steps along the board. If they say *learner/£500*, move them two steps. And if they say *pro/£1,000*, move them one step.
4. You, the adult, are the 'chaser', so your figure always starts at 1. Explain that the idea is that your kiddo has to get the correct answer to move forward, and with each go your figure will also move forward one step at a time. The aim for your kiddo is to keep ahead of you and not get caught by you, which

happens if your player moves on to the same number as them on the board at any point in the game.

5. Set the stopwatch or timer to ten seconds. You read one of the sentences aloud (so your child cannot see the words) and then start the timer/ stopwatch.

6. You both have ten seconds to select which **their**, **they're** or **there** you think was in that sentence and pick up your button.

7. Each time, make sure your child selects their button first, and you obviously will always select the correct answer afterwards.

8. To reveal the answer, read the sentence again and hold aloft the correct answer button.

9. If they were correct, they can move forward one space along the board, and so do you.

10. If they are incorrect, they stay where they are and your figure moves forward one space, getting closer to catching them.

11. The idea is they have to reach the end of the board without being 'caught' by you.

You can make this more physical by making yourselves the figures, and drawing the game board and buttons in chalk on the floor. (You stand on the button to select it.)

HIGH FREQUENCY WORDS RESOURCES

As I mentioned on page 120, **DECODABLE** words are ones that your child should be able to sound using phonics, and **NON-DECODABLE** words are 'tricky' ones that they just have to recognize.

PHASE 2

DECODABLE

a	can	
at	dad	
it	and	
is	had	
in	him	
got	his	
on	has	
an	but	
not	big	
get	back	
up	if	
mum	off	

NON-DECODABLE

of*
as*
the
to
I
go
no
into

* Though lots of people list **of** and **as** are decodable, I think these two words are non-decodable, because they're usually said out loud as **/ov/** and **/az/** – not **/off/** and **/ass/**.

PHASE 3

DECODABLE

will	now	be
with	down	was
that	look	my
this	too	you
then		her
them		they
see	**NON-DECODABLE**	all
for	he	are
	she	
	we	

PHASE 4

DECODABLE
children
went
its
help
from
just

NON-DECODABLE
when
one
what
little
there
have
come

were
like
so
some
said
do
out

PHASE 4

DECODABLE
don't
old
I'm
by
time
house
about
your

day
made
came
make
here
saw
very
put

NON-DECODABLE
oh
their
people
Mr
Mrs
looked
called
asked
could

You can find the full list of all 200 high frequency words at the end of the government's *Letters and Sounds* document. You can find a copy of it online at www.gov.uk/education/phonics

ARE YOU STILL READING THIS?

So that brings us to the end of the reading chapter, which appropriately involves a lot of reading! If you found it all a bit hefty and confusing, don't worry – it's a lot to take in.

When I taught reading and phonics, it took me years to get to grips with everything – and I was doing it daily. When teachers are first thrust into classrooms in their early training, they often admit to feeling daunted by phonics, and some who teach older kids have even confessed to me that they don't really know much about phonics at all. When kids learn this stuff, they are taught it over years. It isn't for us as grown-ups at home to **KNOW IT ALL**!

This information is indexed at the back of the book too, so that when phrases are mentioned by your child's school or a teacher or a fellow adult you can grab this book and flick through to find an explanation, and hopefully a game to match. It's here to guide you as your little one grapples with phonics, to give you a broad understanding and to hopefully inspire you to come up with ways to play and make phonics fun at home.

It doesn't have to feel big. Supporting your kiddo to read can be as simple as popping up some Post-it notes around the house with high frequency words on, or grabbing flash cards to flick through while you're waiting for your other kid to put their shoes on. It can be reading with them every day. It can be looking at road signs together. Five minutes at a time is plenty. They won't need us for long, believe me. Before you know it, they will be reading fluently and when you show them the kids menu and say, 'There is only ice cream for dessert,' (because it's £1 a scoop) and they reply, 'No, there isn't – you can also have sticky toffee pudding or marshmallow sundae or chocolate brownie!' (all stupidly expensive), you'll curse the day you sat down with them and read that first book! HA!

WRITING

SPELLING

LEARNING TO WRITE

ARGH, WRITING!

With Ewan, asking him to write is like trying to get a cat into a bubble bath. There's always a struggle, often loud protests and usually someone ends up wet (with tears!). Ewan, like many children, is very active. He favours constructing things, or firing vehicles down ramps, or running around. Writing is not his bag.

You might even be wondering whether kids today are even going to need to know how to write! How often do you sit down to craft a letter by hand? I write birthday cards and a 'To Do' list on paper (frequently adding to it and rarely ticking off!) but otherwise everything else is done on my phone or computer. It seems quite old-fashioned to work on our penmanship, doesn't it?

YET HERE WE ARE.

Ewan's at school now, and daily writing is suddenly something that has entered our world. Homework is always writing – and, to be quite honest, there have been times when I haven't even battled with him. I've just explained to his teacher that he wasn't up for it and we played a game instead that related to the task at hand. Teachers are a very understanding bunch, I've found, especially when it comes to kids under seven. If you are making an effort to support your children with their learning from home, then teachers are usually delighted. I talk more about building teacher–parent relationships on page 12.

For some little ones, however, writing notes and stories is their idea of fun. How wonderful if your child finds the joy in this! Encourage that all you can. But if you've got a little one who gives you the look of someone who's been offered dog-turd pie for dinner when you ask them to write their name on Granny's birthday card, then it can be tough.

When I was home-schooling through the 2020 coronavirus pandemic, Ewan's enthusiasm for any kind of writing activity dwindled to zero. (Mummy's enthusiasm for ANYTHING also sat firmly at zero by the end!) We played lots of the games that I'm sharing in this chapter. They all worked well for a time, but often he'd become savvy to my stealthy education through play and would outright refuse to engage. (Of course, I followed my **GOLDEN RULE** so the activities sometimes lay untouched for days on end!)

I spoke to his teacher on the phone, and do you know what she said? 'Don't worry.' So, I pass these words on to you here. **DON'T WORRY**.

If your little one is battling with forming words on paper and, if you can face it, make it fun by playing some of these games. But if it makes you feel cross and frustrated, just leave it. There's always tomorrow to try something new. In some countries – Finland and Poland, for example – children don't even start school until they are seven. Part of me understands why. If you look at an X-ray of a child's hand, you can see that their bones don't fully develop until they are seven years old, which could explain why some children find putting a pen to paper so difficult, especially if they have fine motor skills challenges. Patience is our friend here.

So, yes, writing might suddenly become a skill that seems urgent, but try to remember that you can do lots of things to support your little ones with their writing skills without even getting out a pen or paper.

Playing with building bricks, pegs, sand, play dough and mud, threading beads, buttons or dried pasta – anything that gets their fingers working is massively beneficial. These activities are building up muscles in those little hands that will be needed for writing. And colouring in, drawing and painting aren't to be sniffed at either, especially if your little one isn't keen on writing actual words. All these things are helping them to practise fine motor skills while having fun at the same time.

Don't forget, too, that for some children a form of reward might work really well in motivating them. Getting points or stickers on a chart, to get something they really want, can be the magic that ignites the spark. I've sometimes found telling Ewan that time spent writing equates to extra time doing something else he loves. So, for example, fifteen minutes of writing means fifteen extra minutes playing a computer game. (You know your child best.) I try to play one five-minute game for every morning or afternoon my kids and I are at home. The more you and your little folk play the games from this book together, the more you will get to know which ones are likely to be a big hit – the ones that will make their wee faces light up and make you feel like you're winning for a moment.

See, here's the thing: if you are *trying*, then you are brilliant. It is really all we can do, isn't it? Children are simply little humans who have their own very real emotions and moods. There are no guarantees as to what will work. It's all just trial and error – and the trial bit is what really matters, if you ask me.

castle rain

powdered

dragon's blood

Drainage work is taking place

Find the

Potion making always has the advantage of buying me some peace – kettle ON!

If you have a younger child, make them their own potion tray (without the bicarbonate of soda and vinegar), so they can play while their older sibling experiments. You can also give them a pen and notebook to scribble in.

POTIONS LESSON

One lazy weekend afternoon Ewan was watching TV and found a Harry Potter film while flicking through the channels. He became riveted and started asking me questions. As a huge Harry Potter fan (I'm a Hufflepuff, thanks for asking!) I wanted to squeal with delight at his interest, but I tried to act casual, as nothing puts a six-year-old off faster than a parent being keen on it. After the film finished, I explained that I actually had the book that the film had been made from and asked Ewan if he fancied reading it at bedtime. He did, and we are now two books into the series, reading a few pages each night. Here's a game we played to harness the love of all things magic.

GRAB:

- ◼ a tray
- ◼ some cups or pots
- ◼ bicarbonate of soda (a tablespoonful will do)
- ◼ vinegar (a few tablespoons)
- ◼ any other random things as potion ingredients (see below for some examples)
- ◼ spoons or mixing utensils
- ◼ paper and pen

TO SET UP . . .

1. On the tray, lay out cups containing each of your potion ingredients. When I did this, I had five pots: one with bicarbonate of soda, one with vinegar, and, in the rest, blue-coloured water, water beads and blackcurrant cordial. But you can use whatever you like and have to hand.
2. Write labels to give the ingredients magical names. I had powdered flies, frog juice, witches' brew, beetle eyes and golden wizard (this one looked like wee – I love me a 'mum joke'!).
3. Pop out more pots for mixing, and spoons. Leave the pen and paper nearby.

TO PLAY . . .

1. Your child has to experiment to find the two ingredients that make the magical fizzing potion. This is the vinegar and bicarbonate of soda, but they don't know that.
2. Ask them to write down the two ingredients they are going to test. Once they've done that they can put them together in a cup and then either tick or cross if it makes the magic.
3. Hopefully they write down a few before they get the winning combo, and perhaps continue to experiment even after they've found the fizzing potion.

We use a clipboard to lean on, as we often play lying on the floor – my kids are usually more keen to write when they aren't sitting formally at a table, so a clipboard is worth having.

At the end, go through their list and tick them all off. It's always satisfying to see a lovely line of ticks.

GRAMMAR DETECTIVE

In my first book, *Give Me Five*, I shared a game called Book Detective where your little one has to find a letter on the cover of a book and tick it off a list. Letter-hunting became too easy for Ewan, so I needed to find a game for him while his sister (who was four at the time) was playing Book Detective with me. I looked at the **SPAG** stuff on our school website for inspiration and here's what I came up with! (**SPAG** stands for Spelling, Punctuation And Grammar, and it's something that all schools focus on.)

GRAB:

- 5 books
- pencil
- paper
- magnifying glass (optional)

TO SET UP . . .

1. Write '**GRAMMAR DETECTIVE**' at the top of the paper.
2. Draw three columns on the paper and write these headings at the top of them: **ADJECTIVES**, **NOUNS** and **VERBS**.
3. Write the numbers 1 to 5 or 1 to 10 (depending on how long you want to play) down the left-hand side of each column with a tick box to the right.

TO PLAY . . .

1. Place the paper on the floor with the books out.
2. Remind your little one what an **ADJECTIVE** is (a describing word – like yellow, soft, furry, bright), what a **NOUN** is (a thing – toy, ball, bike) and what a **VERB** is (a doing word – like walking, ran, hopped, grabbed).
3. Ask them to choose a book and open it. Can they find any of these types of words on the page?
4. Say 'I can see one' to prompt them. If they're finding it hard, give them a clue: 'It starts with G' or 'It's describing the boy' or 'What is the elephant doing?'
5. When they find one, write it down. Can they find five or ten of each in the book?
6. If your child is a competitive sort, perhaps set a five-minute timer for each type of word. Can they find them before the timer goes off? Maybe write your own list and see if you can go up against them. Who can find the longest adjective? Or the most verbs? Quite often it's simply the fact that you are doing it with them that makes them want to play.

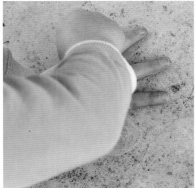

You could also do this with shadows outside on a sunny day, or with a windowsill with toys and a sheet of paper.

IT'S ME!

Kids are so self-absorbed, aren't they? They love telling you about themselves, or showing you their latest trick. '**WATCH THIS . . . LOOK AT ME!**' is something we regularly hear, but there are times when it's hard to muster the enthusiasm to watch them jump off the sofa yet again. So I decided to use this fascination with themselves, and what their bodies can do, to my advantage and encourage the kids into some science without them even realizing it.

GRAB:

- if you have a floor that you can write on with chalk, you don't need anything except chalk – however, if you don't, you'll need . . .
- two large pieces of paper or cardboard (a roll of wallpaper or flattened-out cardboard boxes can work well too)
- masking tape to stick the paper or card together
- pens or pencils

TO SET UP . . .

1. If you're using paper or cardboard, stick the pieces together so that you have one big piece that's roughly the size of your child, and one that's about the same size as you.

TO PLAY . . .

1. Get your child to lie down and draw around them on the floor (with chalk) or on the paper or cardboard (with a pen or pencil). Then they draw around you in the same way.
2. Ask them which part of their body is their favourite and label it. Label your own parts.
3. If you're struggling to get them involved, write funny things or draw a funny face on the head.
4. Depending on what your child prefers, you could aim to draw all the features on the face and body, closely matching their real features, or they might prefer to draw some fun features instead. Let them decide.
5. If they are just drawing and colouring but not writing, don't consider it a loss. Continue to label your own body parts to model the game while they draw; the fact that they have chalk or a pencil in their hand is a win – writing practice doesn't always have to be words.

Of course, you don't need to use technology. If you are keen to get out for a walk, then do it the old-fashioned way and post the quiz questions through your friend's door. Everyone loves getting post!

Each term, teachers tend to focus on a new topic in class. You could do a quiz with grandparents, family or friends for each topic your child is doing at school.

VIDEO QUIZ

During the lockdown periods of the Covid-19 pandemic some of our friends got really into quizzes over online video chat. So much so that even their kiddos joined in, and one family sent us a video of their little girl Penelope asking Ewan some quiz questions – and he loved it! Especially because he knew the answers to three of the five questions. Ah ha! I thought. A golden opportunity! 'Why don't you do a quiz back to her?' I said. So we sat down together and thought about some of his favourite facts from books we had. He wrote out five questions and then we made our video to send back. The last question was his favourite joke!

GRAB:

- pen
- paper
- smartphone

TO SET UP . . .

1. For Ewan, it was better if the other person sent the video first; so if you think your little one would be the same, ask a friend or relative they like to send a mini quiz first, with a request for them to reply with their own quiz!

TO PLAY . . .

1. Together with your child write four questions and one joke on a piece of paper.
2. Then write the answers on another piece of paper or the back of the one with the questions.
3. Record a video for the questions, then another video of the answers.
4. Send to a friend.

VARIATION

- Instead of a quiz, you could also try a fun Q&A (for example, '*What's your favourite dinosaur?*' or ask '*Would you rather*' types of question).

MESSY RECIPE CARDS

Quite often I see messy play or people making stuff online and all I think is **NOPE**. I know I'm not alone here. However, a friend of mine, Myriam @mothercould, who I met through the wonder that is Instagram, has a knack for sharing super-easy recipes for messy play. I watched her for months thinking, *It can't be that easy, can it?* Then one quiet day, when I had enough energy (coffee), I thought I'd give one a whirl. And – well, I'll be blown – she was right! They were simple and easy and made with stuff I could grab during a weekly supermarket shop. So below are two of my favourite recipes of hers. But here's the trick: in order for us to make them, the kids need to write out the ingredients and method!

(Myriam lives in the USA so I've given both the American and English measurements here. I have a set of measuring cups, as I find them quicker to use than faffing about with scales!)

GRAB:

- pencil
- paper or white card
- measuring cups or kitchen scales
- mixing bowls
- spoons
- clingfilm or a ziplock bag
- ingredients as noted below

INGREDIENTS FOR SLIME:

- 55g or ¼ cup of chia seeds
- 400ml or 1¾ cups of water
- a few drops of food colouring
- 360–480g or 3–4 cups of cornflour

INGREDIENTS FOR PLAY DOUGH:

- 125g or 1 cup of flour (tap the cup to get the air out)
- 140g or ½ cup of table salt
- 2 tbsp of cream of tartar
- 1 tbsp of cooking oil (any will do but I prefer to use grapeseed oil, which doesn't have a strong smell)
- 236ml or 1 cup of boiling water
- food colouring or a herbal teabag to colour the water (it's especially fun if you mix up the teabags so the colour will be a surprise!)

TO PLAY . . .

1. Talk your kid through the ingredients and write or draw them out together.
2. Once they've done the initial mixing, put the play dough or slime to one side and tell them it needs to set before they can play with it. While it sets, help your child to write down or draw the steps of what they did. (For the slime, this can be done while it's in the fridge overnight.)
3. Once they've completed their recipe card, it's ready to play with.

TO MAKE THE SLIME . . .

1. Mix the chia seeds, water and food colouring together and leave the mixture in the fridge overnight.
2. The next day add the cornflour a bit at a time, until it reaches a slimy consistency that doesn't stick to your hands.
3. After you finish playing, keep the slime in the fridge. Add a little more water if it goes too firm. We played with ours for a week.

TO MAKE THE PLAY DOUGH . . .

1. Mix the dry ingredients together first. Kids can do this.
2. Then add the oil and coloured water. A grown-up needs to do this as the water will be hot.
3. Let the mixture cool and then knead it well to bring all the ingredients together. Remember it'll be hot because of the water, so make sure you touch it first to check that it's cool enough for little hands.
4. The play dough will be fine to be used for about six months if it's kept wrapped in clingfilm or a ziplock bag in an airtight container.

For messy play, I often lay out newspaper so I can scrunch it up and pop it in the recycling bin afterwards to minimize the mess.

These recipes are taste safe (not edible but fine if they put it in their mouths) so if you have little ones who still put stuff in their mouths they can play with these too.

Younger ones can play too. Florence, who was four at the time, told me what she wanted her letter to say; I wrote it down and she signed her name.

OWL POST

If you've got *Give Me Five*, you might remember Teddy Zip Wire (page 181, if you're wondering). Well, this is like an upgrade of that with a magical twist. In fact, this is the game that encouraged the most writing from Ewan, despite his usually incredible reluctance to put pen to paper. With Owl Post, he actually kept writing to send more and more messages to our friends and family!

GRAB:

- some paper
- a pen
- a hanger
- string
- stickers (optional)
- tape or Blu-Tack
- pegs

TO SET UP . . .

1. Draw an owl that's roughly the size of your hanger and stick the drawing on it. Pop pegs on the hanger or the owl's feet.
2. Write an example letter to somebody. Use stickers (if you have some) to close it, and write a magical address on the front.
3. Leave paper, stickers and a pen nearby.
4. Tie string from somewhere high to somewhere low. I tied it to an upstairs window and to our slide in the garden below, but absolutely anywhere that goes high to low will work too.

TO PLAY . . .

1. Start the game by hanging the owl at the top of the high end of the string, attaching the example letter to the hanger with the pegs, and sending the owl down the line to your child. (Or you can leave the owl at the bottom of the line and wait for your child to find this mystery letter.) Read the address and letter together.
2. Encourage your little one to write a letter. A magical one! To a Harry Potter character, to the fairies, to a naughty troll, to the Christmas elf – whoever they like.
3. Attach the letter to the owl using the pegs.
4. Send the letter down the zip wire to deliver it.
5. I waited at the bottom while Ewan wrote mystery messages to me or our family members and then sent them down with the owl.

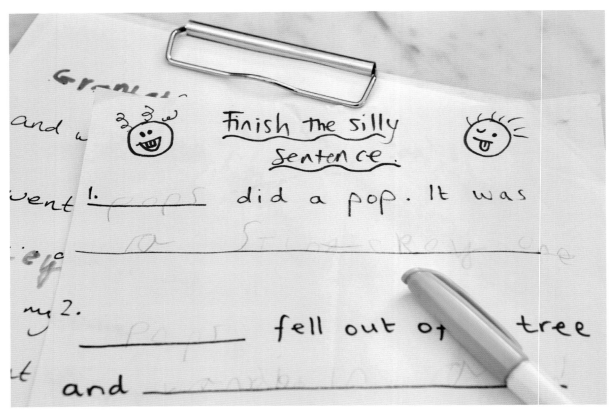

Finish the silly sentence.

1. _____ did a pop. It was

_____

2. _____ fell out of tree

and _____.

This is also a great opportunity to remind your kid about starting sentences with a capital letter and ending them with a full stop.

SILLY SENTENCES

I sometimes wonder if there's a sliding scale with children, whereby the less they tantrum about not getting their own way as they grow from toddler to child, the funnier they find poo, bums and farts. The 'humour' definitely ramps up a notch when they're about four years old, and at times I feel like all I hear the entire day are jokes and discussions about poo, poo-heads and willy-bums, until I reach the point where hiding in another room is the only option. Well, kids, if it's so flipping funny, you can flipping well write about it. HA!

(Joking aside, this is a great game for reluctant writers, because having gaps to write in a word or two is a lot less daunting than writing out whole sentences.)

GRAB:

- ■ a pen
- ■ paper

TO SET UP . . .

1. On the paper write five silly sentences with gaps. Here are some examples:

- ■ .... fell off the .... and went ....
- ■ I went to the toilet and .... and it was so ....
- ■ One day my bum .... and it went ....
- ■ .... did an enormous pop and it smelled ....
- ■ Mr Poopy-Pants was .... so he went to the .... and ....

You get the idea!

TO PLAY . . .

1. Read the words in the sentence together. If your kids aren't sure how to fill in the gaps, give them a few ideas for answers that are outrageous and hilarious (according to them). Then say, 'I won't look while you fill out the rest,' and see if they take the bait.

2. Remember to heartily laugh at their answers! You could even have a go at seeing who can write the funniest sentence.

3. When you've completed all the sentences, or exhausted silly words for the gaps, ask your child, 'Want to make your own silly sentence?' If they do, winner! If they don't, that's OK too.

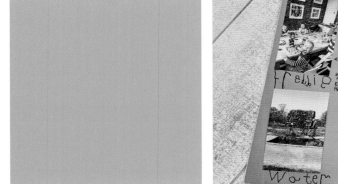

PASSION PROJECTS

This isn't so much a game but some ideas to encourage children to write by using things they already enjoy. Ewan and Florence love cracker jokes. Every Christmas we read the jokes out of the crackers we pull and then the kids 'entertain' us with their own 'jokes'. I'm sure you can sense the eye rolls and fake laughing from where you are. But, because they enjoy it so much, we all participate, which leads to all the grown-ups attempting to teach them really cheesy jokes! So one day, in order to encourage Ewan to write, I suggested he wrote his own joke book.

TO MAKE A JOKE BOOK . . .

1. Get two sheets of A4 paper and hold them together, one on top of the other.
2. Keeping them together, fold the sheets in half.
3. Pierce two holes through the fold in the middle.
4. Get a piece of string and thread it through the holes and tie the ends together, to create a book.
5. Leave your child to write one joke per page and draw a picture for each joke.
6. Encourage them to write a silly title on the front and draw pictures on the cover.

HERE ARE A FEW OTHER IDEAS, BUT THINK ABOUT WHAT YOUR CHILD LOVES THE MOST AND BE LED BY THAT.

- Make their own comic book or graphic novel.
- Write down clues for a treasure hunt around the house for parents or siblings to follow.
- Print out some photos of things you've done recently and make a scrap book with captions to explain what they are doing in the photos.
- Search for famous sporting events (goals or medal wins) on YouTube and get them to write the commentary. Watch a 'top ten moments' video together and challenge them to write down a description of one of the events they've just seen and see if you can guess which one they are writing about.
- Write riddles about objects in the house. Take it in turns to write a mysterious description and see if the other person can guess what it is. For example, You must put me in your mouth every day but you don't eat me – what am I? Answer – a toothbrush! They can be super simple; just make sure you pull out your best Oscar-worthy acting to string out the guesses!
- Write out a menu for a three-course meal they would like to prepare or eat.
- Write a Christmas or birthday list using a toy catalogue or website.

Giving my kids access to my laptop can be such a novelty for them that they're often keen to write by typing on the keyboard. If you search 'Guided Access' online, you can find ways to lock your computer so your child only has access to specific programs, and can't accidentally order twenty-five coconuts, which turn up on Thursday at midnight!

PEN PALS

It's all a bit hi-tech these days, isn't it? I can't imagine my kids meeting another child on holiday now and swapping addresses so they can write letters to each other with actual pen and paper. I mean, I'm sure perhaps some do, and how lovely, but I'm pretty certain most will just say 'Text me' instead! So what other ways can we use writing to get messages to each other? Here are four ideas.

YOU'VE GOT MAIL

Set your child up with their own email address and then ask relatives and friends if they want to write to them. Kids often are more excited to write back if they get to use your computer to type on.

DOODLE

Get a 'doodle' app for your phone or tablet. Write a question to your child on it – for example, What would you like for breakfast? – and ask them to reply by writing their answer.

SECRET MESSAGES

Sit down with pen and paper in front of you. Ask your child to sit behind you and write a word (spelling words or tricky words they are learning at school would be great here) on your back with their finger. You copy their movements with the pen and paper and see if you get the word correct. Then swap places and you write on their back. What funny words (or squiggles!) come out?

SPY WRITING

Write a note on white paper in white wax crayon. Give your little one a bit of water with a touch of paint or food colouring in it to paint over the page and reveal the message. Can they write back with their own secret message?

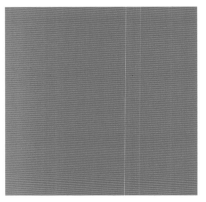

To make it more challenging for older children, you could reduce the time or say that you only get points for getting a word that no one else has got. Or play it as per the TV show and the longest word wins.

COUNTDOWN

Just this word makes me think of the ticking clock track on the TV show! When I was a teenager and at secondary school, at the end of every day I would walk home, have a hot chocolate, and me and my mum would watch *Countdown* together. Recently it was on when Ewan was home and he started trying to spot words in the letters on the screen, so I said, 'Shall we make our own version?' And we did!

GRAB:

- any letters (at least 20) – they could be magnetic letters, letters on bits of paper or Scrabble tiles
- 2 bags of any kind
- a pen
- paper
- a timer of any sort (you can use the *Countdown* clock on YouTube if you like!)

TO SET UP . . .

1. Separate the letters into vowels and consonants.
2. Place the vowels in one bag, and consonants in the other.
3. Set the timer for one minute for little ones, or thirty seconds for older kids.

TO PLAY . . .

1. Take it in turns to pick nine letters from the bags, making sure you have a mix of vowels and consonants.
2. Lay the letters out in a line, then start the timer.
3. See how many words you can make out of the nine letters and write them down. (This is where it differs from the TV show. On *Countdown* the game is to make the longest word, but I find that it's more encouraging to make as many words as possible.)
4. Compare your words at the end and count each time a letter is used to see who got the most points. So if you wrote down *an*, *it*, *son*, *nit* and *tan* you'd get thirteen points.

HANDWRITING

Can you remember doing this at school? I can. For a period of time I insisted on drawing a little heart for each dot over an *i* or *j*, which was ridiculously time-consuming.

Handwriting is something that children will be learning and practising from their first year at school. Some schools teach children cursive writing, which is a way to write letters that encourages joined-up writing – an example of cursive writing is below.

However, not all schools do this, or they teach it later on, so don't worry and ask the school if you aren't sure. Now, I've always found writing quite a personal thing, so, although I encourage my children to write as the school tells them, I also let them be creative with their letter formation because, well, sometimes, the way you do something just feels easier to you and that's fine in my book. This is especially the case when it comes to left-handers. There are plenty of things you can buy to support left-handers, such as special pens and pencil grips, and even entire books on the subject. Here are a few fun ideas so your kids can practise handwriting at home, whichever their dominant hand is.

MAKE YOUR OWN WIPE-CLEAN WRITING BOARD

When forming letters, children can get very frustrated and cross when they get it wrong, and this can put them off continuing to try. However, using wipe-clean boards or books can help reduce this frustration. Being able to instantly erase what they've done means they're more likely to try again, in my experience.

To make your own wipe-clean board, simply put wide sellotape smoothly over a piece of cardboard to create a shiny surface. Then use a dry-wipe pen or chalk pen to write on to it. You can even write templates on to the cardboard before you put the tape over the top, for your kids to follow the lines.

PANGRAMS

Pangrams are sentences that include every letter of the alphabet, so they are a good way to practise writing. Here's the most famous one:

The quick brown fox jumps over the lazy dog

But there are many others. Here are two more child-friendly ones:

The five boxing wizards jump quickly

How vexing quick daft zebras jump

It also helps if a child's feet are touching something when they write, so smaller chairs or being propped up to sit comfortably can make a huge difference when it comes to writing practice.

A good tip I was given to encourage writing is to have a 'writing area' somewhere in your home. An old cup with some pencils in and access to paper or a notebook left in view should be enough to entice a curious child.

WHO NEEDS A PENCIL?

Getting creative by writing in lots of different ways is something I often do with my kids. Here's a handy list of the many things you can use instead of a pencil.

- Get some bath crayons and scribble as they scrub.
- Write with your finger or a kitchen utensil in a tray of shaving foam.
- Write on masking tape in rainbow colours.
- Write with a biro on a banana skin – so satisfying!
- Write on cardboard with a paintbrush and water.
- Use chalk on floors that are easy to clean.
- Use a whiteboard marker or chalk pens on windows or glass doors.
- Write a letter as big as you can on a large piece of paper and make it get smaller and smaller in a line. How tiny can it go?
- Cover a piece of firm card with kitchen foil and use a blunt stick (like a chopstick) to indent letters in it.
- Write on to a tray of salt, flour or glitter (then find glitter in every crevice for months after!).
- Give your child a special pen and writing notebook. It's amazing how having something like this can make them more eager to write.

FINGER SPACES

When learning to write, children are encouraged to put their finger after each word to leave a space. There is a knack to this, though, because we don't THINK in finger spaces, do we? When writing, we just think of a constant stream of words, so remembering to pause between each one can sometimes take a bit of brain training. Here are my top tips to help:

- **Do a daily sentence.** Every day, sit together to write one sentence. Start with a three-word sentence and build up by a word a week over three or four weeks. Spend five minutes sitting with them to do it, reminding them each time to include finger spaces, as well as full stops and capital letters. Make the sentences funny if you like!

- **Use tiny toys or small bricks instead of fingers.** Write sentences together on a large piece of paper and pop a toy between each word. Sometimes having something physical to move into place can help.

- **Silly Sentences on page 145** can also be useful. Write some of your own silly sentences, but without spaces between the words. Then give your child a different coloured pen or highlighter to draw a straight or wiggly line in a different colour or highlighter to show where the spaces should be.

SPELLING

Usually when your child is around age five or six (Year One in the English school system) they start to bring home spellings. These are a list of words they must learn how to spell, and then they take part in a weekly 'test' at school to see how well they have learned them.

Obviously each school varies how they do this, but in my experience there is often a similar format and it falls on us, the adults they live with, to teach the kids to learn how to spell these words at home. Yikes!

Many schools I've worked in, and my children's school, offer a 'Look, Cover, Write, Check' sheet that goes home with the words they are to learn. This is a piece of paper for the kids to learn the words by looking at them, covering them, and then writing them in one list and checking to see if they got the spellings correct. Now, if you have a child who comes home from school, gets out their homework, asks to do it, then diligently follows the instructions on a daily basis, memorizes the words perfectly in this format, then scores 10 out of 10 each week on the test, this method is excellent. That's if you're the parents of Matilda from Roald Dahl's classic story!

For everyone else with non-fictional children (that's me and you), this is not how it will go. So my first task each week is to rip up that 'Look, Cover, Write, Check' worksheet and pop it in the recycling. I don't find it helpful. It's boring. And (if I haven't banged on about this enough yet, then I am clearly not doing a great job) as we know, kids learn best through play! Especially at this age.

The other reason I don't like worksheets like that (now, don't get me wrong: if your kid loves those sheets, brilliant – go ahead!) is because we all learn in **DIFFERENT** ways. Our differing brains are what makes each of us unique and wonderful. Not everyone learns by covering and writing and checking. Some do, but lots won't. Some children find words hard to understand, or writing hard to do, or they need to understand the meaning before their brain will retain the information. To cover all these bases we can play games that give each child the best chance of memorizing those words and the order of the letters. In fact, the more unusual ways we can play with those words, the better – and the more chance we will be hitting the exact thing in your little one's brain that goes, *Ah, yes* – **GOT IT!**

WHY DO THEY DO SPELLINGS?

One of the most important things our education system is teaching our kiddos is how to write. How to communicate clearly by writing down words. When you think about it, pretty much every exam they will ever do to determine 'how well they have learned something' is based on how well they can retain information and then write it down. Learning spellings is a very early form of this. Children are given information to go away and learn; they have to try to memorize it, and then at a later date retrieve that information from their brains and write it clearly down on a page. So, yes, although we all have a spellcheck function on our phones and computers, this process of learning is what our kids are really practising when they're learning their spellings. For them to succeed through the education system, doing this effectively will be extremely helpful. However, that doesn't mean that the way they do it has to be so boring and stressful that it makes you want to drop-kick a dictionary through a window!

> After you are done with the spellings for a week, keep hold of the words you created in a bag or box, as they can come in handy for other games whenever you need them.

WHY THESE WORDS?

Out of all the words there are, why are they learning these? Well, it's up to the school, but teachers in England follow a national curriculum that gives them sets of words to cover for each age group. These are often **HIGH FREQUENCY WORDS**, which are the ones we will see the most often in everyday life and when reading books, which means knowing how to spell them will be incredibly useful to our children. Many schools also follow the phonics phases, which include certain words that are either decodable (can be read using phonics) or non-decodable (often called 'tricky words') (pages 124–125). As your child goes further through the phonics phases, they will start to learn suffixes (pages 112–113) and prefixes too, which are often taught as spellings.

Some words just never stick in your brain, do they? I always have to check the word 'their' even though I've learned it a thousand different times and write it often. Can you think of any words you always get stuck on? Try to remember this when teaching kids to spell. It's always easy once you've got it, but before then it might as well be written in another language, because that is exactly what it feels like.

Sometimes I use coloured foam instead of card as it lasts longer and I can use it to play more games in the future. I store them all in a zip wallet afterwards. You can get the foam online, and zip wallets in most supermarkets.

MY FIVE MINUTE MUM SIX-DAY METHOD

So, having thrown away the dreaded worksheet, how do I go about the learning of spellings? Well, we have a week to learn each set. We never do homework on a Sunday because that's a day to relax. (Ha! Kids? Relax?) So that leaves me with six days a week. I split the week into three.

- Two days are for five-minute activities where we just read the word and **UNDERSTAND** it, and learn to recognize the ones we aren't sure about.

- The next two days we play games where we **CONSTRUCT** the words using letter games.

- The final two days we actually find ways to **WRITE** the words down.

But, before we do any of that, I get the spellings list and I write each word out on a piece of coloured card. Nice and clearly. I put a rubber band around them and stick them on the pin board or fridge ready for easy access. Sometimes I write them out twice so I have two sets, because, as you'll see from some of the ideas in this chapter, I often need another set of the words. You'll need these **SPELLING WORDS** in lots of the games in this chapter.

Every day, either before school (my kids get up super early so we sometimes can grab five minutes before getting dressed) or after school, we spend five minutes on spellings. And how do we do that? **WE PLAY ...**

UNDERSTAND

So, as I explained above, for the first two days we **READ** the words and get familiar with them. We **UNDERSTAND** them and talk about them, and we play games to help us recognize them. There are a few different things we can do during those first two days when we have a new list of spelling words to learn.

Don't forget, of course, it is only **FIVE MINUTES** a day. That is plenty. Don't make this a chore that you all dread.

Another important element is to praise your child's effort. Don't just say 'well done' when they are correct; praise them when they're trying to remember the spelling or write the letter. It's just as important to have a go, even if they get it wrong. Say things like 'I love how you tried to sound that out.' The key is to encourage the effort!

So here are some things you can do first with your lovely set of words . . .

1. Ask your child to flick through the words you've written on the cards and put them into two piles – ones they find easy and ones they find hard.

2. Ask them to tell you a sentence using each word. Then you repeat the word back in a sentence of your own. Make the sentence as wild and silly as you can. So, for example, if the word was *sat,* **you might say, 'The purple horse sat on the green poo!' This is where you can also pick up on their understanding of the word. Do they know what it means, and can they use it in the right context? If not, help to model the word using examples.**

3. Place the words on the cards around the house. Put one on each step of the stairs so your child can step on them and say them out loud as they go up to bed each night. Or pop them where you have meals or where they brush their teeth – or anywhere you will be together every day so you can just point to them and read them.

4. Look for word patterns. Do they all have similar endings? Or certain sounds in them? How could you chunk words – it's easier to remember chunks than individual letters: for example, 'ing', 'er', 'at' and so on. Use a highlighter pen or underline the chunks to point them out. Or cut the words up and swap the endings around. Perhaps put them into category piles – all the ones with 'er' on the end go here, for example.

5. What rhymes with the words? Can you make up a short funny poem with the words? For example, if the word was bridge, you might say: 'The girl couldn't get to her fridge. She had to build a bridge.' It doesn't have to make sense – just be as silly as you like and maybe do a stick-man doodle to go with your rhyme, and then your child might fancy joining in.

6. Can they find the words in a book? Get out a few of their favourite books and a magnifying glass (or an empty loo roll) and be a word detective. Can they spot the words and show you where they are? I often sit with my kids and read ahead, giving them clues if I can see

The games on **pages 164–169**, as well as those with the **star symbol**, will all help your child to understand the words they need to learn, and hopefully have some fun at the same time.

CONSTRUCT

So after the first two days of just playing one quick five-minute game a day that involves reading the words, we move on to the next two-day stage.

This is where we start to construct the words. We don't write them just yet; instead, we play around with letters and build the words in different ways. On occasion, though, when life has got in the way, and we haven't done any spelling work all week and then Friday swings around, I've been known to play these word-construction games with Ewan and he was still really happy with how he did in his weekly test. This is because I always want the process and fun of playing to be the main reasons we do our five-minute spelling games. Ewan's confidence and enjoyment at this stage in his education is more important than scores on a weekly spelling test, because I'm trying to build a love of learning.

Now, just a quick word about spelling tests. The teachers at our school write the results for that week's test at the top of the new words sent home to be learned the following week. They also write the words the child has spelled incorrectly, which I find very useful to know. I always sneak a quick look at these results but rarely mention them to Ewan. I don't want the focus to be on the test and what he got right and didn't.

The result simply helps me to know if what we were doing at home was useful to him or not, but – unless Ewan asks or talks about it – I don't mention the test. There are years to come where test results become important. For now, though, I'm happy to just use the spellings as an opportunity for a five-minute game.

Some schools put a huge emphasis on spellings and highly reward children who get them all correct. For me, I don't find this massively helpful for all children. I'm sure there are some who are motivated by this, but I feel that it can lead to added pressure on kids who are likely trying their best already. I am very lucky that my children's school provides the perfect balance.

I prefer to see the tests as a helpful tool for teachers to understand how well the children can retain the information, and therefore put in place support for those who regularly struggle. If children are naturally good at spelling, the rewards are already there, as writing will come easily to them in an education system designed to praise that skill. I think what I'm really trying to say here is that spellings aren't the be-all and end-all. So, even if the school your little one is at thinks they are so important, the best way we can ease the pressure at home is by making it as fun as we can – using games that suit the way our little ones learn and that zone in on their interests, whatever they may be. If your child is struggling, and you're worried about dyslexia, please see pages 18–19 for more information.

WRITE

Finally over the last two days, usually Thursday and Friday morning for us, we do some form of writing. Now I say writing, but it actually is still playing in a way, because it's never pencil and paper in our house - although, obviously, if that's what you've got to hand, that's absolutely grand. There are lots of ideas on how your little one can practise their fine motor skills in 'Who Needs a Pencil?' on page 155.

You could write sentences on bits of paper with the spelling words missing for your little ones to place the correct word in the correct sentence. But obviously that takes more than five minutes so I rarely bother!

SPELLING WORD AIRPORT

It is amazing how long a paper aeroplane can keep my two occupied. They have also been the cause of MANY arguments and sibling fisticuffs. 'Whose plane is best?' and 'Who ruined whose plane?' consistently make the top ten of the Reasons For Squabbling chart. Still, we can't let that stop us when it comes to five minutes of educating fun, can we? Otherwise we'd never do anything. So, this game is one to put those pesky planes to good use.

GRAB:

- paper
- 10 books
- flash cards of spelling words (see page 7)

TO SET UP . . .

1. Make a paper aeroplane.
2. Lay the books around a room with one spelling on each book. These are your airports.

TO PLAY . . .

1. Each child has a paper aeroplane.
2. They have to throw the planes and get them to 'land' at the airports.
3. When a plane touches any part of a book, the child can collect the 'passenger', which is the spelling. They have to read the word to allow the passenger on the plane.
4. Once read, they can tuck the word into the plane and fly it back to base – which is sometimes a laundry basket, or sometimes my kids just launch it at me. Whatever gets them laughing!

Collect eggs for all the kids and write something appropriate on each. When Florence was three she had the letters of her name on her egg shells to smash, while Ewan had his spelling words.

Alternatively you could hide the egg shells around your garden or home, and the kids have to run around to find the word – which means they burn off some energy too . . . as long as you don't mind bits of egg shell everywhere!

I always scatter the leftover shells on my plants to deter slugs from eating them! Garden hack!

EGG SMASH RELAY

This isn't a game of my invention but I want to include it here because it is played so often by me and the kids. My lovely friend Susie, who owns Resolve to Play, often runs hashtags on Instagram so that people in the play community online can share their ideas. This egg-smashing idea is one that I first saw on those hashtags and has since done the rounds multiple times on many play accounts, though it's a mystery where the game originated. So here is how I use it for spellings.

GRAB:

- flash cards of spelling words (see page 7)
- at least 10 egg-shell halves (when you've cracked an egg for a cake or omelette, rinse out and keep the shells)
- a marker pen
- a tray
- something to smash the eggs with (toy hammer, wooden spoon)
- goggles (optional)

TO SET UP . . .

1. Write the spelling words on the egg shells.
2. Pop them on the tray at one end of a room, or even better the other end of your garden if you have one.
3. At the opposite end, lay out the spelling words face down.

TO PLAY . . .

1. Your kids have to choose a word, turn it over and read it.
2. Then they run to the eggs and smash the correct one.
3. Keep going until they've smashed all the egg shells!

bench
bench

paint
paint

think

paint
paint

You can do this for anything. See how I play pairs for numbers with Domino Match-up (page 195) and Clock Pairs (page 251).

SPELLING PAIRS

As you may have noticed, I play this game a hundred times with so many things in so many ways. So it isn't an exciting new game, but it's one that is always useful and that the kids enjoy. I'm popping it here to remind us all that games can be simple and super easy. This is one I often use on a Friday, before I shove some beige freezer food into the oven and pour myself a cocktail!

GRAB:

- 2 A4 pieces of card, the same colour
- pen
- scissors

TO SET UP . . .

1. Fold one piece of card in half, then half again and again. Unfold it to reveal eight equally sized sections.
2. Do the same for the second piece of card. Then write eight spellings words on one, and repeat on the other so they're identical.
3. Now cut out each word so you have sixteen spellings words, and lay them face down, mixed up on a table.

TO PLAY . . .

1. Take it in turns to turn over two word cards.
2. As you turn over each card, say the word aloud to help your child read along and encourage them to do the same.
3. If your words match, you keep the pair.
4. If they don't match, return them to being face down.
5. The winner is the one with the most pairs once all the words have been matched.

After they've got the word, they could squirt it off the wall with medicine dispensers or water pistols!

FOAM ANAGRAMS

As I mentioned earlier in this chapter, I sometimes write the spelling words on thin foam. You can get this from pound shops or craft shops, and it's really durable and handy to have for all kinds of games. The main reason it's so good is because, when it's wet, it sticks to lots of surfaces like glass, tiles or shiny kitchen surfaces like cupboard doors, dishwashers and fridges.

GRAB:

- craft foam
- permanent marker
- scissors

TO SET UP . . .

1. Write the spelling words on the foam and cut them out.
2. Then cut them out into individual letters but keep the words together. I use our old bath-time stacking cups for this but you could make little piles or pop them in any small containers.
3. Put them in the bathroom.

TO PLAY . . .

1. At bath or shower time, as your kid is soaking in the tub or rinsing in a cloud of steam, hand them a cup which has the letters of one of the spelling words in.
2. They then use the water to stick the letters on to the bathroom wall so they can see the letters they have.
3. Tell them the word that these letters should make. Help your child to move the letters around on the wall to make up the word.
4. Then hand them the next cup of letters and repeat the game until all the words have been spelled out.
5. Afterwards, you could keep the letters on the wall and see what other words (or even sentences!) they can create by moving them around.

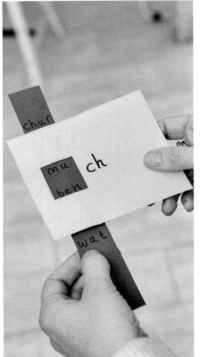

Spelling words could be stuck up around the house as fun word reminders.

GET CRAFTY

For some children the idea of sitting at a table cutting and sticking really floats their boat. If your little one loves this sort of thing, try some word play with these crafty ideas.

WORD COLLAGES

GRAB:

- flash cards of spelling words (see page 7)
- safety scissors
- old magazine or newspapers
- glue stick
- paper or thin card

TO PLAY . . .

1. Place the spelling words in front of your child.
2. Together, cut out the letters that you need to spell them from the magazine or newspapers.
3. Recreate the words by sticking them on the piece of paper or card.

LETTER SLIDER

GRAB:

- paper or thin card, of 2 different colours
- scissors
- pen

TO PLAY . . .

1. Cut two lines to make a slot in a piece of paper, as shown in the photo opposite.
2. Write the recurring letters on this paper.
3. Make a strip of paper that fits into the slot.
4. Write the alternative letters on the strip.
5. Slide it up and down to show the different words.

CONNECTION GAMES

All you need to play these two games is paper and a pen. That's why I love these ones so much, because I can set these up in one minute and leave them for the kids to do while I'm cooking their dinner. Five minutes of spellings done with minimal effort. Now, if only a nutritious meal my kids will actually eat was as simple to prepare . . .

SPIDER'S LETTER WEB

GRAB:

- pen
- paper

TO SET UP . . .

1. Divide the paper into sections using the pen.
2. Within each block, write the letters from one of the spelling words randomly around the space.
3. Put little circles around each letter as shown.

TO PLAY . . .

1. Your child has to connect the letters in the correct order to spell the word.
2. The lines to connect them will criss-cross within each section, making a 'web'.

If you want to make this game harder, you can. Just write all the letters from the spelling words randomly all over the page without dividing them into blocks.

MISSING LETTER

GRAB:

- ▪ pen
- ▪ paper

TO SET UP . . .

1. Write each word down the left-hand side of the sheet of paper with one letter missing.

2. Draw a line where the missing letter should be, as shown in the photo below.

3. On the right-hand side of the page write all the missing letters but in a mixed-up order.

TO PLAY . . .

1. Your child has to draw a line from the word to its missing letter.

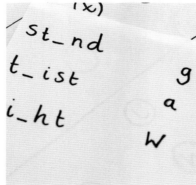

If you want to make the Missing Letter game trickier, simply have multiple missing letters.

For younger siblings, make up their own tray with the letters of their name for them to put into the correct order so they feel like they're joining in too!

If you own one of those letter light boxes or boards, you can use them instead of magnets on a tray.

BOX OF LETTERS

If you have a set of letters to play with – wooden, or magnetic or plastic – then these are some ideas of how you can get the most out of these for spelling practice.

PLAY-DOUGH STAMP

GRAB:

- a pot of play dough (if you have the time to make this, see pages 140–141 – it can be a fun joint activity)
- a tray
- some letters
- flash cards of spelling words (see page 7)

TO PLAY . . .

1. Squish the play dough out flat on the tray.
2. Use the letters to stamp out the spelling words.

MAGNETIC SPELLING

GRAB:

- a metal baking tray
- magnetic letters – but only get the letters needed for the words to be spelled (too many letters can be overwhelming)

TO PLAY . . .

1. Scatter the letters around the edge of the tray.
2. Ask your child to build each word in the middle.

HOP, SKIP AND JUMP GAMES

These are for physical learners. For some children this is the only way they learn – through movement. During my time as a teaching assistant, I would often be asked to take a group of children who were finding words tricky out of the class to give them some extra support. The first thing I usually did was walk right past the table allocated for me to work with them and go outside where there was space to run and jump. This is where I'd see the real progress happen.

JUMP TO IT

GRAB:

- marker pen
- coloured card or paper (or, if you have them, large foam mats or card with letters on)
- flash cards of spelling words (see page 7)

TO SET UP . . .
1. Write the letters needed as large as you can on the card.
2. Scatter them around the space you're playing in.

TO PLAY . . .
1. Shout out the word and they have to jump into the correct letters to spell it out.
2. You can mix it up with hopping to the letters, too, if you like.

LETTER SPRINT

GRAB:

- any form of letters – magnetic, plastic, or bits of paper with letters written on (you only need the letters required to create the spelling words)
- timer (optional)

TO SET UP . . .

1. Pop the letters at one end of a large space.

TO PLAY . . .

1. Shout out a word.
2. Your little one has to run and grab the letters needed for that word as fast as they can.
3. They return back to where they started and form the word.
4. Set a timer for competitive kids.

You could set up two identical sets of letters and make it competitive if your kid loves to try to beat you.

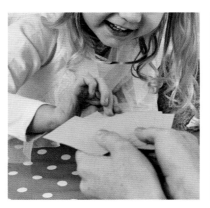

Use a stopwatch and see which word they can make the quickest. Can they beat their own best score?

GET ARTY

If your little one would rather daydream and doodle than practise the order of letters in a word, then perhaps use some of these ideas to encourage a combination of the two.

GRAB:

- flash cards of spelling words (see page 7)
- pen
- paper
- colouring pens or pencils or paints

PICTURE MEMORIES

1. Write down each spelling word on a piece of paper.
2. Ask your little one to draw a picture of something that reminds them of that word.
3. It can be anything at all – part of a silly sentence or just an image that flies into their head when they think of it.

BUBBLE WRITING

1. You write the word in bubble writing and your child finds ways to colour it in or make patterns within the letters.

SHOUTING MONSTERS

1. Fold an A4 piece of paper in half and then the outer edges back on themselves as shown in the photos opposite.
2. Write the word in the middle of the first fold with a speech bubble around it. Alternatively, you can write the word in a speech bubble on a separate bit of paper and cut it out.
3. Your child can then create a monster on the outer folds of the paper. If you've got a separate speech bubble, stick it on to the picture at this stage. (See the photo opposite for an example of ours.)
4. When you pull the folds apart, it will look like the monster is shouting the word!

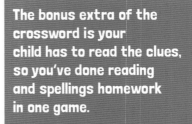

The bonus extra of the crossword is your child has to read the clues, so you've done reading and spellings homework in one game.

CLASSICS

These two classic word games might seem so obvious, but when I realized this was something I could do to make spellings more interesting, it was a revelation! **OF COURSE!** Why didn't I think of it before?! So I quickly squiggled some of these down on bits of paper and I felt like I had really made an effort without actually doing much. That is what I call a win and definitely an occasion to crack out a Creme Egg. Now, I'm sure you don't need me to explain either of these, but just in case . . .

WORDSEARCH

1. Draw a grid on a piece of paper.
2. Write the words randomly around the grid.
3. Sing '**A, B, C, D . . .**' as you fill out the rest of the spaces on the grid. (Singing optional!)
4. Write the words that need to be found down the side, with a tick box for when they have been found. (Kids love a tick box!)

CROSSWORD

1. Write your words out in straight lines, across and downwards, so they criss-cross each other on common letters. This will be your answer grid – don't let your kid see it!
2. Copy the grid but without the letters inside the boxes.
3. In the blank grid, give the box at the start of each word a tiny number.
4. Write the corresponding number and a clue down the side or under the grid. The clue can be a sentence with the word missing or something super simple like: **IT RHYMES WITH 'SAT' AND BEGINS WITH 'M'**.
5. Alternatively, if you're short on time, give the clues verbally (so your kiddo can concentrate on spelling the answer, rather than reading the clue).

What else could you use in your house to build the words?

If they are competitive, set a timer and see how fast they do it, then see if they can beat their time the next day.

ORDERING GAMES

The process of simply ordering the letters to create the words we need to spell can be all it takes to make spelling seem more interesting. These are the spelling games Ewan enjoys the most. He enjoys constructing, so anything that taps into this joy he will join in with! If you know what makes your child tick, then that's half the battle won! Here are some of the ways we construct our spelling words, using bits and bobs we often have around the house:

- Write the letters on the side of DUPLO® or LEGO® bricks and make word walls.
- Cut up empty toilet-roll tubes and write letters on them. Use a kitchen-roll holder or a broom handle to put the letters on and construct the words vertically.
- Write letters on ball-pit balls and use a muffin tin or cups or cupcake cases to hold them to create the words.
- Give old baby building blocks a new lease of life by writing letters on the side and building word towers.

THE WASHING LINE

Another way to order the letters is to use a washing line. You can either use masking tape as your washing line, or a string and some pegs. Just set up a line between two chairs at your child's height.

TO SET UP . . .

1. Cut the spelling words written on bits of paper up into individual letters and mix up the order of the letters but keep them in word piles.
2. Set up your washing line. If using masking tape, make sure the sticky side is facing you.

TO PLAY . . .

1. Get your child to unscramble the anagrams. You can prompt them by saying which word it is.
2. They need to put the letters on the washing line in the correct order to make the word.

To encourage them to write out the spellings during these games, for games 2 to 5 just get a piece of paper and pencil for them to write down each word as they 'win' or reveal it.

If you're taking turns in a game, you could write down the spellings too. But write them with errors and see if your child wants to mark you work, showing you where the mistakes are. Great for confidence!

OLD FIVE-MINUTE GAMES REIMAGINED

These are some of the games I still play from my first book when we're learning spellings at home. They're all recognition games, so would usually be played on the first two days of my six-day method (page 159). However, you could easily add ways to write the words too, so you could play them on the fifth and sixth days as well.

1. TREASURE HUNT

Hide the spelling words around the house. Give them a list to cross out the words they find. You can offer 'hot' or 'cold' clues if you like and ask them which words they're still looking for from their list.

2. THE TRAP

Lay out six cushions on the floor and pop one spelling words on top of each. Then select one word and tell your child that word is the 'trap' – they have to read the words to find the trap. If they step on the trap word, you 'catch' them. Once done, remove the trap word and choose another word to be the trap. They keep travelling along the cushions until you run out of words. (The point of the game is to get them to read all the words and recognize the trap word.)

3. CRACK THE EGG

Put the words inside bits of foil and then wrap that foil in play dough. They have to undo it all to discover each word and read it out loud.

4. REACTION WALL

Pop the words on a wall somewhere, and give your child a spatula or something to hit them with. Set the timer for one minute – during this sixty seconds you shout the words and your child has to find them and whack them as fast as they can. Then you take a turn so they are reading the words out.

5. STEPPING STONES

Again, pop the spelling words next to six cushions, then your child can roll a dice and jump along the cushions based on the number rolled. They read out and collect the word next to the cushion they land on. Keep rolling until all the words are collected.

WRITE IT OFF

There may seem a lot in this chapter of writing and spellings, but remember it's simply one thing for five minutes. The reason there are so many things to try is because when kids get bored, that's when they lose interest and the chance to learn is limited. If we can keep mixing it up, the more likely we can hold their attention long enough to wedge a bit of education into the fun! Plus they will always have a favourite and, once you've found that, milk it for all it's worth!

I also want to make a note here about mistakes in writing. When our children are first learning letters and sounds, they will frequently spell things 'incorrectly' (according to us grown-ups) even though they are technically phonetically correct. So, for example, they might write: 'Wee went throo the masiv chree to fighnd a seecrit dor.' Translation: 'We went through the massive tree to find a secret door.'

This sentence is a fantastic example of a child who is really doing well at learning phonics. They have sounded out the words by breaking them down and chosen to represent them on paper using the letters they know that make those sounds. Now, because English doesn't perfectly follow those phonics rules, it isn't technically correct, but we shouldn't jump in and immediately tell a child this.

The first thing to do here is to praise what they've done. What a wonderful sentence. How exciting. I wonder what's behind the secret door? Focus entirely on the positives. Our main aim is to build confidence and encourage them to keep writing. Teachers are hugely skilled at correcting written work in a way that keeps them motivated.

If your child is confident enough in their writing, you might want to help them with a few words that they might see frequently. So you might say, 'Ah, I see you've used the "**igh**" here to make the "**eye**" sound in "**find**". How clever. But the "**eye**" sound in the word "**find**" is made using just the letter "**i**". So shall we write it out again together? **F-i-n-d**. There are lots of ways to make the "**i**" sound.'

Also reiterate, whenever you correct your child's work, how hugely difficult language can be, even for grown-ups, and that everyone makes mistakes all the time. Never cross out what they have done; instead write the word correctly next to it or on another bit of paper if they seem willing to know.

Some children can get very frustrated at being corrected, and become disheartened. It's totally understandable. I once taught a child who had very carefully spelled out the word 'night', only for me to then explain that the knight he actually was writing about had a silent 'k'. When he threw his pencil down in disgust, I wanted to join him. Sometimes English is just a total headache! The trick is to try as hard as you can to laugh and be silly. To treat it like a game, a code to be cracked, and to have patience with the little ones in front of us who are trying to get to grips with it all.

Like I said before, it can feel a chore at times, but once your child finds the freedom of expressing themselves through written words, the most beautiful things can happen. They come home with notes written to you, or their friends. They might form the letters that spell out '**Igh Luv Yoo**' on a bit of paper and you'll put it in a box to treasure forever.

MATHS

NUMERACY, NUMBERS, SUMS . . .
WHATEVER YOU WANT TO CALL IT . . .

DOMINO MATCH-UP
CHALK OBSTACLE COURSE
SNACK-TIME TOMBOLA
ORGANIZATION STATION

NUMBER BONDS
- PUZZLE BOARD BONDING
- HANDS DOWN
- BUILD A BOND
- SUCK IT UP
- BOND BOOGIE
- MAKE THE TEA

SPLIT THE DECK
REVERSAL LADDER
THE DROP
CAR TARGET
THE MAGIC TOWEL
DOTTY DICE

TIMES TABLES
- VIDEO GAME MATHS
- THE THREE TARGETS
- GRIDBLOCK

OLD FIVE-MINUTE GAMES
REIMAGINED

NUMBERS IN A NUTSHELL

MATHS
NUMERACY, NUMBERS, SUMS . . .
WHATEVER YOU WANT TO CALL IT . . .

I feel like the age range I am trying to support with learning games in this book takes us up to the absolute limit of my capacity for maths! I am not a numbers person. If someone asks me to work out a sum on the spot I feel like I have the icy trapped wind of Elsa (Queen of Arendelle) in my gut. The cogs in my brain start creaking like an old clock and all the numbers jumble up in my head. I once worked on a strawberry field as a teenager, collecting the money for pick-your-own days. I cannot tell you just how many people were given a made-up amount of change because I couldn't instantly deduct the price of their punnet from the cash in my hand! However, despite this, I managed to pass my maths GCSE with the support of an incredible teacher (Mr Lovelady, thanks) and, even though it was my lowest GCSE grade, it was the result I was most proud of, because it did not come naturally.

The reason why I am telling you this is because I think it is really important when we are doing anything at home that is educational with our children, that we try to remember a time when we found it impossibly hard ourselves.

It is so vital that we do our best to recall the emotions we felt and put ourselves in the shoes of the little humans in front of us who are trying to learn. As adults, we don't often willingly put ourselves under the pressure to learn something completely new, because it seems so daunting to start at the beginning. Yet our kids are doing that every day, and it's essential to remind ourselves of the toll this can take on energy levels and emotions.

So, on to the subject of maths . . . There are a few different things that our kiddos will be learning when it comes to numeracy in their first couple of years at school. I have gathered together my favourite games to support this. Fun is always the desired outcome for any of these games, so it's not crucial to play them daily, but I hope that gaining confidence in using numbers is a by-product. And, if nothing else, I use these games myself to get back into the swing of times tables, mental addition and subtraction, and all the other bits and bobs I regularly did my best to avoid at school.

These games roughly follow your kiddo's progression in learning maths, and I've also popped in sections to focus on number bonds and times tables too.

MATHS GLOSSARY

A lot of the terminology for maths will be familiar. However, I still think it's useful to have a reminder. And, as always, some things HAVE changed. I've done my best to provide explanations, although goodness knows it's tricky. Old habits die hard!

SUM:
This word is used to ask for the 'total' and is rarely used to talk about maths in a generic way (for example, 'Did you do your sums?'). Teachers nowadays are more likely to say, 'What is the sum of all those numbers?' And kiddos will know they are asking for the total of those numbers added together.

NUMBER SENTENCE:
This is the phrase that has replaced the general word 'sum'. A number sentence is simply a mathematical sentence such as:
$3 + 2 = 5$ or $7 - 5 = 2$.

NUMERACY:
This is a word that refers to using maths in real life, such as arithmetic to work out change in a shop. It's the term that lots of schools now use instead of simply 'maths' for this important subject.

NUMBER BONDS:
These are pairs of numbers that make a certain total number. These are explained in more detail (with examples) on pages 203–205.

TENS AND ONES:
In my day (I feel like a grandma when I say this!) we used to say 'tens' and 'units'. But now teachers tend to refer to 'tens' and 'ones', so 27 has 2 tens and 7 ones.

DIGIT:
I think we all probably know that a digit is just a number, but teachers often use this term when teaching our kids maths, so it's handy for us to also use it at home.

MULTIPLE:
This is the ANSWER number to times tables. So the multiples of 5 are 5, 10, 15, 20 and so on.

MULTIPLIER:
This is the number of the times table you are working on. So if you're going to work on your 6 times table, the multiplier is 6, because you're multiplying all the numbers by 6.

DOMINO MATCH-UP

The first few games in this chapter are for children who are just beginning to learn their numbers. When your little one starts school, they will focus on learning and recognizing numbers up to 20, being able to count backwards and forwards, and understanding the value of each number. By 'value', I mean knowing that the number 3 on the page matches three items. This is one of the games I played with Florence to help her get to grips with this concept.

GRAB:

- dominoes
- pen
- paper
- scissors

TO SET UP . . .

1. Grab as many dominoes as you think your little one might be interested in.
2. On a piece of paper, write the number of dots on each domino, side by side.
3. Cut out the numbers to match the dominoes as shown in the photo.
4. Lay out the numbers and dominoes for your child to find.

TO PLAY . . .

There are two ways to play this:

1. They can try to match the correct written numbers with the number of dots on the dominoes and put them in little pairs together. Flo and I said they had found their twin and were off to the park.
2. Or you could play **PAIRS**, by turning the written numbers and dominoes over and spreading them out so you can't see any of the numbers or the dots. You take it in turns to pick up one of each (a written number and a domino) and see what's on the other side. If they match, you keep the pair. If they don't, you put them back, face down. Keep playing until all the pairs are found.

If you don't have an outdoor space, you can do this with masking tape through your house. We have created an obstacle course through our kitchen and lounge this way before.

Obviously the numbers on the stepping stones can change based on their capabilities. They could be counting backwards from 20 to 10 or even counting in 2s, 5s or 10s and so on if they already learned times tables.

CHALK OBSTACLE COURSE

During the 2020 lockdowns, we created a little obstacle-style course drawn with chalk on the pavement outside our house. It had a **START** line, and I drew stepping stones, as well as arrows pointing backwards and symbols for hops, twirls and star jumps – all the way along to the **END** line. The stepping stones and the chalked instructions were like obstacles because they slowed you down as you did your best to race to the end line. One by one, our neighbours took turns to try it and then we'd text each other our best times! The kids have since asked for a course regularly so I decided to add some numbers to it and do a bit of stealth learning as they hop, skip and jump around!

GRAB:

- chalk
- any stretch of pavement
- timer (optional)

TO SET UP . . .

1. Write **START** on the ground. Follow it with any challenges you like.
2. Make sure that two of the challenges you include in your obstacle course are stepping stones. Draw lots of circles big enough for feet to step into, with numbers written in them. You can do as many number stepping stones as you like. Write the instructions **COUNT FORWARD** on one of the stepping-stone obstacles and **COUNT BACKWARDS** on the other.

TO PLAY . . .

1. Do a demo run yourself to show the kids how it's done. Do the course and count out loud as you jump on the numbered stepping stones.
2. Each child then gets a practice go.
3. Then it's time for the proper run! You could run alongside, supporting by counting with them if they need help. Encourage them to cheer for each other as they go.

You can play this game with number sentences too. Pop a maths question on the tickets instead (3 x 2 = ? or 1 + 4 = ?) and make sure the answers match the food items you have.

Sometimes for fun (for me!), I put foods they aren't keen on in the tin too so it becomes a snack roulette! You never know – they might just try those bits of 'dreaded' cucumber if they 'win' them.

SNACK—TIME TOMBOLA

I don't know about you but I get incessant requests for snacks. Florence says 'I'm hungry' every fifteen seconds when at home. She once said 'I'm hungry' as she was eating – it's such a reflex response! You probably know by now what I do when my kids are obsessed with something . . . I turn it into a game! This game is a snack-based one, so I can finally get a bit of respite from the relentless requests!

GRAB:

- a muffin tray
- a variety of small snacks – different cereals, small berries, dried fruit, or whatever your child likes that is age-appropriate
- paper
- scissors
- a container

TO SET UP . . .

1. In each hole of the muffin tray put a different number of the snacks. So you might have one chocolate button in the first, two raspberries in another, three Cheerios in the next and so on. Some good snacks we have used include raisins, grape halves, breadsticks, tiny crackers, little cubes of cheese, peas and sweetcorn, raw carrot sticks . . . You get the idea.

2. On bits of paper, write numbers that match the number of items in each bit of the muffin tin. Cut them out, fold them up and pop them into the container.

TO PLAY . . .

1. When your little one says they're hungry (and you're happy for them to have a snack) grab the container and say, 'Roll up, roll up! Choose a ticket and see which snack you have won!'

2. Your child has to choose a ticket from the container and see what number it is.

3. Then they have to find which hole has the same number of items in it – and your child gets to eat the contents of it! So if they pulled out a 3 they would get to eat the three Cheerios.

4. They will definitely ask to choose another ticket immediately!

We like to do 'tournaments' in our house with the cars or weights. Go to my website fiveminutemum.com to see more about my competition set-up. (It's a great way to encourage writing too!)

ORGANIZATION STATION

Some really brilliant skills that you can teach your little one through play are ordering, categorizing and pattern recognition. These three things can be done in hundreds of different ways – every time you sit with your child and separate a puzzle out into colours, or line up their teddies in order of height, you are actually teaching them the thinking skills that they will need for numeracy, which will come in hugely handy at school. Bonus! Here are some ideas, but let your imagination run wild and, as always, be drawn to what your child loves the most.

1. CARS
Send toy cars down a slide or ramp on to a sheet of paper and mark how far they go. Can your child line them up in order of distance travelled?

2. SCALES
Make your own scales with a clothes hanger, some string and two cups or buckets. Get lots of toys and see which is heavier and lighter and have a mini competition to see which item wins the heavyweight title! Or pop a large toy in one side and see how many smaller toys are needed to match its weight.

3. STICK MEN
Draw loads of stick men, all different heights, on a bit of paper. Cut them out. Can your child put them in height order?

4. COINS
Gather a big handful of change. Can they put the coins that match together? All the 1p coins in one pile and the 10p coins in another? Can they put them into size order from biggest to smallest?

5. PATTERNS
Get toys that you have a lot of – cars, blocks, colouring pencils – and see if you can show your little one how to make a pattern. Car, block, pencil, car, block . . . What comes next? Can they see the pattern? Can they make their own?

NUMBER BONDS

If you have a child in reception (their first year at school) you might have heard the term 'number bonds'. A bit like when I first heard the word 'phonics', this for me was another 'WTF is that?' moment. I furrowed my brow and tried to remember if this was something I had done at school. Fractions? Multiplication? Yep, those sound familiar, but **BONDS**? **WHAT ARE THEY?** Sometimes they are called 'number pairs' too, just to throw you off a little more. **HA!** Isn't being a parent of school-age kids **FUN**? Always something new to try and grapple with. But don't worry. As with lots of stuff we hear casually dropped into conversation around the school gates, it's a lot simpler than it sounds. Number bonds/pairs are two numbers that are added together to make a target number.

FOR EXAMPLE, THE NUMBER BONDS TO 10 ARE AS FOLLOWS:

$$1 + 9, \quad 9 + 1, \quad 2 + 8, \quad 8 + 2, \quad 3 + 7, \quad 7 + 3,$$
$$4 + 6, \quad 6 + 4, \quad 5 + 5, \quad 10 + 0, \quad 0 + 10$$

When added together, they make 10, and so they become a pair or bond. For 10, there are six pairs of numbers that our little nose-miners need to learn, and, although it is pretty obvious to us, your little ones also need to understand that the numbers can go both ways.

So, **6 + 4** and **4 + 6 BOTH equal 10.**

Well, that's easy, innit? You can also do bonds to 5 and bonds to 20. Learning these is a great way to support your child's mental arithmetic, as well as helping with their understanding of patterns and how numbers work. Some kids get these pairs quite easily and can quickly grasp it. Some others might struggle and it can take seeing the pairs being demonstrated with lots of different methods to really get the hang of it. Either way, I've got some fun ideas and games to help play with number bonds at home.

The games I've played on the next few pages (206–211) all use number bonds to 10 as an example, but you can, of course, adapt them all for any other bonds or pairs you like. To help you out, on the next couple of pages I've written out the number bonds to 5, 10 and 20.

NUMBER BOND RESOURCES

NUMBER BONDS TO 5:

1 + 4
4 + 1

2 + 3
3 + 2

5 + 0
0 + 5

NUMBER BONDS TO 10:

1 + 9
9 + 1

2 + 8
8 + 2

3 + 7
7 + 3

4 + 6
6 + 4

5 + 5

10 + 0
0 + 10

NUMBER BONDS TO 20:

1 + 19
19 + 1

2 + 18
18 + 2

3 + 17
17 + 3

4 + 16
16 + 4

5 + 15
15 + 5

6 + 14
14 + 6

7 + 13
13 + 7

8 + 12
12 + 8

9 + 11
11 + 9

10 + 10

20 + 0
0 + 20

PUZZLE BOARD BONDING

If you have wooden puzzle boards like the one in the picture opposite, try to keep hold of them. As tempting as it is to throw out baby toys once your children have grown out of them, open-ended toys like this with numbers, letters and even just pictures will come in handy for a lot longer than you might first imagine. (By 'open-ended toys', I just mean toys that can be played with in lots of different ways, like blocks, bricks and vehicles.) If you don't have a puzzle board, you could recreate the idea below with a piece of card and some sticky notes very easily.

1. Cut out bits of paper with the numbers 0–10 written on them and pop them under the number bond on the puzzle board – so the paper number 1 goes under the number 9 puzzle piece, the paper number 2 goes under 8, and so on.
2. Ask your child to try to guess what is under each puzzle piece to create 10 before they lift it up.
3. Alternatively tip the puzzle pieces out of their holes and let your little one put the correct number into the hole first, followed by the puzzle piece with the correct number on it to make the number bond to 10.

HANDS DOWN

Obviously when it comes to number bonds to 10 our own hands are our best tool. Saying 'What's the pair for this?' and then holding up your own fingers is an easy learning game you can play with them when waiting in a queue.

1. Help them to draw around their own hands on a sheet of paper. Let them cut them out.
2. Stick only the wrists and palms of the cut-out hands on to another sheet of paper. (Don't stick down the fingers as you need to be able to fold them.)
3. Fold the fingers down and write numbers 1–10 on the reverse of the fingertips from left to right.
4. On the other side of the fingertips, write the numbers 1–10 from right to left.
5. Show your child how to use the fingers by folding them down, to reveal the matching pair.

You can also play a combination game for these. With Ewan, we sucked the numbers out of a bowl, and then he had to find the matching DUPLO® tower to make 10.

If you don't have enough bricks, make a tower of 10 and see how many ways you can split the tower in two.

If you've got competitive little ones, turn it into a race with a bowl each for you and them, or with a sibling.

BUILD A BOND

I frequently get asked for games with building bricks because they are so popular with kids and many children would much rather play with them than anything else. So here's how we use our collection of barefoot weaponry for number bonds.

1. Get out a collection of connecting bricks. Make a tower each of 1, 9, 2, 8, 3, 7, 4 and 6, two towers of 5 and one tower of 10.
2. Pop the 10 tower on the table and say your child has to work out how to make five more towers of 10, exactly as you have done, but without breaking up the towers you've already made.
3. If you like, give them a piece of paper so they can write out the number sentence for the number bond once they've found it.
4. Once they've made all the towers, see if they can all be placed on top of each other to make the **BIGGEST TOWER EVER**.

SUCK IT UP

I think we started playing this game accidentally, but, to be honest, I can't for the life of me remember. Sitting here writing this now is making me think I need to play this again with the kids because I can remember it inducing a lot of giggles, which is always the desired outcome. Learning is all well and good, but mostly we just want to have a laugh, don't we?

1. Write the numbers for number bonds to 10 out on bits of paper. Make sure there are two 5s and a 10 and a 0 too.
2. Pop them in a bowl and get a straw.
3. Explain to your child that they have to pick a number out of the bowl and then find its matching pair to make 10. But there's a catch: they can't use their hands!
4. They have to suck through a straw until a bit of paper sticks to the end of it, and they keep sucking until they can get the paper out of the bowl. (And then they can stop sucking!)
5. Look at the number on their bit of paper. Can they tell you what number they need to find to make 10?
6. Once they know what they're looking for, they can use their straw again to see if they can find its matching pair in the bowl.

You could play Bond Boogie with addition too. You shout the answer and they have to jump on two numbers that can be added together to make that answer.

They can make tea for teddies or dolls if they still like role-play games.

Alternatively, you could play together and you add a number of spoons in front of them, counting out loud as you go, and they have to go next to add the correct amount to make 10.

BOND BOOGIE

Have you ever played one of those dance games in an arcade where you have to step on the arrows in time with the screen and music? I am so bad at them but cannot resist popping in a quid when I see one because I am guaranteed laughter. I've tried to incorporate the fun of that game into number-bond learning here. Whack the music up . . . !

1. On twelve A5 (half a piece of A4) sheets of paper write the numbers for your number bonds.
2. Place the numbers randomly in a circle around your kid.
3. Put music on a device that you are able to pause. When the music is playing, your kid can boogie.
4. When you stop the music, shout out a number. They have to put one foot on the number you've shouted and the other foot on the matching bond to make 10. So if you shout, 'Eight!' then they have to jump on 8 and 2.
5. Once they've got the correct numbers, put the music back on and go again. If they like, they can just jump on the paired bonds while the music is on.

MAKE THE TEA

Now, I love a toy tea set, especially because of how long it'll keep Florence happy and quiet. But don't worry if you don't have a tea set – some cups and jugs will do just fine.

1. Get out five cups and use a bit of paper or wipeable marker to number them 5, 6, 7, 8 and 9.
2. Lay out a little bowl with some flour or cornflour in it, a spoon, and a jug or toy teapot filled with water. (Cornflour will make gloop – or 'oobleck' if you want its proper name – when water is added.)
3. Put a spoon or two of flour into each of the numbered cups.
4. Explain to your child that each cup has to have 10 spoons of 'tea' (flour) in total for a perfect cup of tea. The label/number written on each tells them how many spoonfuls are already in the cup. (There isn't that many, of course, but they don't need to know that and this saves additional mess!)
5. They have to work out how many more spoonfuls of 'tea' they need to add from the bowl. And then they can add the water from the jug or teapot and give the 'tea' a good mix to make the perfect cups of tea for everyone!

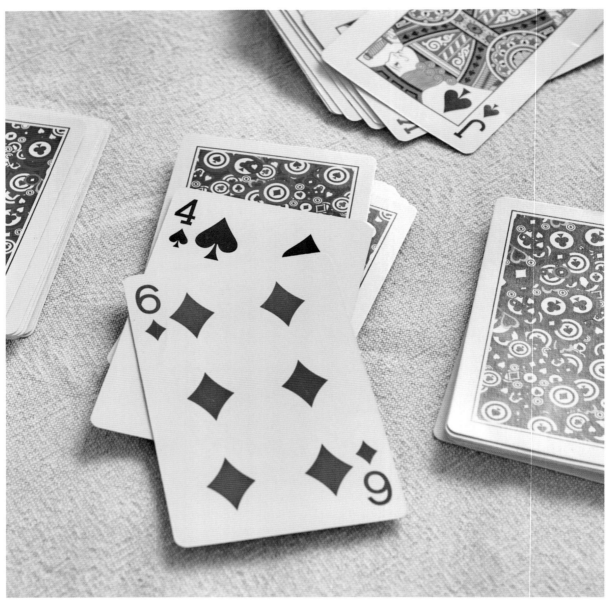

You could play the addition game as subtraction (taking away) instead, which would be a fun way to learn about minus numbers. Or, of course, you could play by multiplying the numbers for a real challenge!

SPLIT THE DECK

Now that we've covered number bonds, let's do some more general maths games! I love games using a pack of cards. It's such a handy thing to always have in your bag for when you find yourself unexpectedly waiting for something with children in tow. When I was a kid we used to go on camping holidays to France and I can vividly remember playing (and cheating at!) card games all the time. I'm hoping that if I play some simple games with my kids now, I can recreate some fond childhood memories with them.

GRAB:

- a pack of playing cards

TO SET UP . . .

1. Remove all the jacks, queens, kings and jokers.
2. Split the deck evenly between the number of players.

TO PLAY AN ADDITION GAME . . .

1. Each player draws two cards from the top of their own deck.
2. Add the numbers together and say the total out loud. (In other words, you have to work out the sum of the two numbers.) For this game, ace equals one.
3. The person with the highest total wins and takes the cards that were drawn by all the other players.
4. Keep drawing two cards at a time and play until one person has all the cards.

TO PLAY A PLACE–VALUE GAME . . .

1. Each player draws two or three or four cards from the pack, depending on how confident your child is with numbers.
2. Line them up in a row and read out the number in full. So if you draw a 3, a 6 and a 2, you would say, 'I've got three hundred and sixty-two.'
3. The person with the highest number wins and gathers the cards from the other players.
4. Keep playing until one person has all the cards.

For little ones, make a ladder with six rungs and use one dice.

But what about the number 1? Keep playing until the number 1 is left, then roll a single dice to get this final number, in order to win.

REVERSAL LADDER

Ewan is a big fan of numbers, which he certainly doesn't get from me! He loves anything that involves maths, and will happily play games where he can spot a number instantly. In fact, when he was younger, in order to encourage him to write, I often played games where he had to write down numbers as I knew it was much more likely he would have a go at this than writing his own name! However, this reluctance to write meant that when he formed numbers on a page they weren't always the correct way round. This is a game we played to practise recognizing which is the correct way to write a number.

GRAB:

- masking tape
- pen
- 24 pieces of paper
- scissors
- two dice

TO SET UP ...

1. Use the masking tape to mark out a giant ladder with twelve rungs on the floor.
2. On the pieces of paper write any twelve numbers you like, but also write the same numbers backwards, as if a mirror was being held up to them.
3. Put one number and its mirror image on each rung of the ladder.

TO PLAY ...

1. Roll the dice and add the dots on them both together (more maths!) to find out what you scored.
2. Jump along that many rungs of the ladder.
3. Pick up ONLY the number from that rung that is the correct way around. If you choose the right one you can keep the number; if you pick up the incorrect one you have to put it back and wait for your next turn to try again.
4. If there is more than one player, take it in turns to roll. Start again at the bottom of the ladder with each new roll of the dice.
5. Keep rolling, jumping along the ladder and collecting until all the correct numbers have been picked up.

THE DROP

There is nothing better than a big box! The best thing about it is that it brings me as much peace as it brings joy to the kids. They love them. We've saved big boxes for days, flattened them, painted on them, built with them. The ideas are endless. For this game, we use a cardboard box and turn it into a giant pinball machine to make adding numbers together a big old game!

GRAB:

- a large sturdy cardboard box
- masking tape
- scissors
- pen
- ball (a tennis ball or similar)
- something to write on (I like to use something wipeable like a mini whiteboard)

TO SET UP . . .

1. Using the tape and scissors, turn your box into something similar to the photo on the page opposite, with edges round it to keep a ball from rolling off.
2. Cut holes in the box (as many as you like) and write a number next to each hole.
3. Pop the box on to something, so it is off the ground (we used a couple of chairs).

TO PLAY . . .

1. Explain to your child that they have to try to roll the ball into one of the holes.
2. You lie under the box, and when you call out 'Go!' your child rolls the ball.
3. When the ball comes through a hole, you have to try to catch it.
4. Your child writes down the number of the hole it went through and then rolls again.
5. They then write down the second number.
6. When they've got two numbers, together create a number sentence. So if the ball went through 1 and 3 you might write $1 + 3 =$ ___, or if it went through 6 and 4 you might write $6 - 4 =$ ___ (depending on the numeracy skills you're working on).
7. Encourage your child to work out the answer to the number sentence.

8. Swap places, and they try to catch the ball from underneath while you write out the next number sentence. (They can help you work out the answer!)

■ You could make a tiny version of this with a cereal box and a small ball if you don't have a large box and you can put your hands under the box to catch the ball.

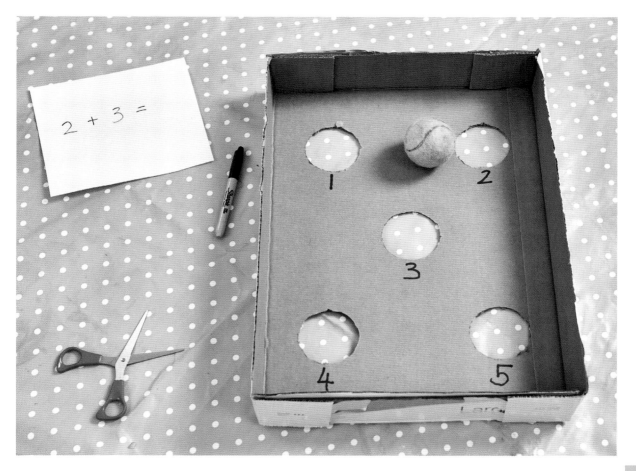

CAR TARGET

If you are looking for a game that you can vary for any age, then this is for you! I trialled this first with people who follow me online and it was a huge hit, probably because it is so versatile. The idea behind the game is that your little one is adding up and taking away over and over without even realizing they're doing loads of maths. If they already love maths, this game might seem like even more fun for them!

GRAB:

- a big piece of cardboard
- paper and pencil
- a marker pen
- 2 different-coloured toy cars
- scissors
- tape to create edges, or something to make a barrier around the edges
- chair (or anything else that's a similar height, like a stool or low table)

TO SET UP . . .

1. Cut the box and tape the edges to create a ramp with a large enclosed landing area that has barriers or edges to stop the cars flying off. (See the photo of ours opposite.)
2. On the landing area, draw a grid with numbers written in the squares. Write whatever numbers you think your little one can manage.
3. Lean the ramp against a chair or similar. Put the cars at the top. Write a target number on a blank piece of paper. We set the target at 50.

TO PLAY . . .

1. Explain to your child that one car is an addition car and if you send that down the ramp it adds up the numbers, and if you choose the other colour car it takes the number away. Explain that the target you are trying to reach is 50 (or whatever you chose as your target).
2. They select the addition car to start with and send it down the ramp. Ask them to write down whatever number it lands on, then roll the car down again. Write down the second number and then they have to add the numbers together. The answer won't have made 50, so help them to recognize that they need to add more numbers and select the adding coloured car again. ➤

TARGET NUMBER!

50

5+5+4...
+6+5
4+9=

Play with different target numbers each time to keep the game interesting.

Lots of people who played along online used blocks to create barriers for the cars. And some kids made the cars out of LEGO® as an extra activity.

3. Your child should keep sending the car down the ramp, and use the pencil and paper to add up the numbers that it lands on. At some point the sum of the numbers will go over 50, so they will realize they need to use the subtraction car to try to reach the exact target number. Eventually (well, that's the hope!) the car will land on the number required to exactly hit the target and they've won!

VARIATIONS

- For very little ones, you could roll the car down and see if they can say what number it lands on. If they have an older sibling playing the game, give your littlest one a go rolling their car and recognizing the numbers in between the eldest one's turns.
- For kids a little older but not ready for number sentences, write the numbers 1 to 5 or 1 to 10 on the landing area and write the same numbers on a piece of paper and let your little one tick them off each time a car lands on that number. Try to see if they can tick off all the numbers.
- If you want to encourage number writing, give them a blank piece of paper to write down the numbers the cars land on. Can they get them all?
- If they are just getting to grips with addition and subtraction, number the grid up to 10 and set the target quite low to start with. You can always increase it as they grow in confidence. Starting with a quick easy win is often the way to go.
- For children who are older, include a multiplication car and make the targets trickier numbers, like 362.
- Because Flo is working on recognizing numbers from 11 to 20, when I played this with her and Ewan, she took turns with her brother to roll the cars. She recognized the numbers, then he wrote the number sentences and worked out the answer. Flo stopped playing much sooner than he did, which didn't matter one bit.
- If your kids are prone to arguing (which is often the case with mine, depending on their mood!) then wait until you have two cardboard boxes and make them one ramp each!

You can use regular pens instead of permanent marker, but the numbers will disappear in the water quite quickly.

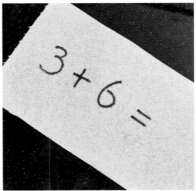

If your kitchen towels won't stay folded over, use a bit of tape to secure them.

THE MAGIC TOWEL

I love discovering something that brings magic alive for children. I never shy away from an opportunity to make them go all wide-eyed with wonder. We have a fairy garden and I tell my little ones stories about naughty elves all the time. My nan did it with me, and I loved imagining the fairies and pixies in the woods getting up to mischief, so I've carried on the tradition. This idea is a way to bring a tiny bit of magic to learning.

GRAB:

- thick kitchen roll or paper towel
- a permanent marker pen
- a shallow tray filled with water
- a magic wand (optional)

TO SET UP . . .

1. Fold a sheet of kitchen roll in half.
2. On the top half, write a number sentence without writing the answer. So, for example, write 3 + 6 = on the left-hand side of the sheet and leave the right-hand side blank.
3. Now lift the flap of the sheet to reveal the side underneath and write the answer only on the right-hand side.
4. Refold the sheet and press firmly so it stays folded and the answer remains hidden.
5. Repeat with as many sheets and number sentences as you like and leave them next to the shallow tray of water.

TO PLAY . . .

1. Ask your child to select a number sentence.
2. Do they know the answer? If they're not certain, help them to work it out using fingers or counting along a number line (see page 8 to create your own number line).
3. Once they are sure they know the answer, pick up the sheet and the wand and say any spell they like. We use 'Numero Revealio'!
4. They can then drop the sheet into the water and the answer should be revealed. Did they get it correct? Choose another one, and swap who says the magic word and who drops the paper to reveal the answer.

DOTTY DICE

Dice are like playing cards. Something super easy and fun you can play with, in loads of different ways, and you might have a few knocking around in the cupboards. Here are a couple of games we play with dice and some LEGO® . . .

GRAB:

- a dice
- 20 toy building bricks and a small toy figure per player
- **OR** a few pieces of paper and a pen, if you don't have any toys to hand

TO SET UP . . .

1. Make a line of twenty 'stepping stone' bricks for each player, with a figure for each player at one end.
2. **Alternatively**, you can draw the stepping stones on a sheet of paper and use bits of paper with your names on for each player.

TO PLAY ODDS AND EVENS . . .

1. Grab a dice and take turns to roll it.
2. If you roll an even number, you move forward that many number of 'stepping stones'.
3. If you roll an odd number, you move backwards that many steps, stopping at the beginning brick if you go back that far.
4. The winner is the first one to get to the brick at the end.

TO PLAY ONE MORE, ONE LESS . . .

1. The same set-up as above using twenty bricks and a figure for each player.
2. Cut out two bits of paper. On one of them write **1 LESS** and on the other one write **1 MORE**. Fold them all up so you can't see what's written on them and pop them in a container.
3. Each player rolls the dice and then picks out a bit of paper from the container.
4. If they get **1 MORE**, they can move one more than whatever number they rolled. If they get **1 LESS** they move one fewer brick than the number they rolled.
5. The first one to get to the brick at the end wins.

TO PLAY DOUBLE OR HALF . . .

1. The same set-up as before with twenty bricks and a figure for each player.
2. This time if you roll an even number on the dice you have to halve it and only move that many spaces. Show your kids how to split the number in half if they need support, by splitting the number of dots into two equal groups (so 6 dots can be divided into two groups of 3 dots, so you can only move forward 3 spaces).
3. If they land on an odd number, they double it and move that number of spaces.
4. The winner is the first one to get to the brick at the end.

To make the games longer just add more stepping stones.

To make the games trickier use two dice so they have to also add the numbers together first.

TIMES TABLES

This is something we probably all remember from school. Well, we remember having to learn them at least. However, I certainly struggle with anything beyond the 8 times table! Luckily for me, I get to live it all over again with my children – what a treat!

I can remember reciting the times tables as a kid, in a monotone voice over and over. I can recall doing tests, and I can picture myself practising them at the dining-room table. I wonder, though, whether the answer to 8 times 6 might have stayed in my head a bit better if learning my times tables had been fun too.

So over the next few pages I've attempted the improbable by making learning times tables as joyful as I can. I tried out a few of these games with Ewan, and whenever he asks to play again I know we have a hit on our hands.

Don't forget too, of course, that the old tricks still apply. Looking for number patterns and creating a grid like the one opposite can be useful as you try to explain that 5 times 4 is the same as 4 times 5. Pointing out patterns – such as adding the zeros for multiples of 10 or that multiples of 5 always end with a 5 or 0 – is a good use of five minutes when introducing a new set of times tables to learn.

For me, the hand trick is a genius way to work out multiples of 9. So, just in case you never learned it or have forgotten it, here it is: hold your hands up with your palms facing you. If the number you want to multiply 9 by is 3, fold down your third finger on your left hand and the remaining fingers will tell you the answer. You've got two fingers to the left of the third finger, and seven to the right, and the answer is 27. It works for all the answers up to 9 times 10 – for 9 times 11 and 9 times 12 you're on your own!

TERMINOLOGY REMINDER

The **MULTIPLIER** number is the number of the times table you are working on. So if you are doing the 3 times table, the multiplier is 3. **MULTIPLES** are the answers. So multiples of 3 would be 3, 6, 9, 12 and so on.

It's useful here to introduce NUMBER FACTS. These are ways of showing how numbers connect in different ways. In the number bonds section I showed that you can have **6 + 4 = 10** as well as **4 + 6 = 10**. Similarly, when it comes to times tables, it is useful to learn how we can reverse **2 x 3 = 6** to get **3 x 2 = 6**. And let's not forget division! We can use number facts to show children that **6 ÷ 3 = 2** and **6 ÷ 2 = 3**.

Number facts simply demonstrate to children that there are different ways we can play around with numbers. This is why grouping games with any kind of small objects (such as toys, counters, dried pasta or cereal – anything at all!) is a great idea. Try to make it physical where possible when introducing times tables for the first time – or using something like the grid opposite can also be a fun way to help kiddos visualize these number facts.

TIMES TABLE GRID

X	0	1	2	3	4	5	6	7	8	9	10	11	12
0	0	0	0	0	0	0	0	0	0	0	0	0	0
1	0	1	2	3	4	5	6	7	8	9	10	11	12
2	0	2	4	6	8	10	12	14	16	18	20	22	24
3	0	3	6	9	12	15	18	21	24	27	30	33	36
4	0	4	8	12	16	20	24	28	32	36	40	44	48
5	0	5	10	15	20	25	30	35	40	45	50	55	60
6	0	6	12	18	24	30	36	42	48	54	60	66	72
7	0	7	14	21	28	35	42	49	56	63	70	77	84
8	0	8	16	24	32	40	48	56	64	72	80	88	96
9	0	9	18	27	36	45	54	63	72	81	90	99	108
10	0	10	20	30	40	50	60	70	80	90	100	110	120
11	0	11	22	33	44	55	66	77	88	99	110	121	132
12	0	12	24	36	48	60	72	84	96	108	120	132	144

When making flash cards, don't forget that, if you want to make division ones, you can write the number sentence backwards and simply change the = to ÷ and the **X** to **=** then you'll have the correct number facts for those too! So **2 x 5 = 10** becomes **10 ÷ 5 = 2**.

1 TIMES TABLE	2 TIMES TABLE	3 TIMES TABLE
1 x 1 = 1	2 x 1 = 2	3 x 1 = 3
1 x 2 = 2	2 x 2 = 4	3 x 2 = 6
1 x 3 = 3	2 x 3 = 6	3 x 3 = 9
1 x 4 = 4	2 x 4 = 8	3 x 4 = 12
1 x 5 = 5	2 x 5 = 10	3 x 5 = 15
1 x 6 = 6	2 x 6 = 12	3 x 6 = 18
1 x 7 = 7	2 x 7 = 14	3 x 7 = 21
1 x 8 = 8	2 x 8 = 16	3 x 8 = 24
1 x 9 = 9	2 x 9 = 18	3 x 9 = 27
1 x 10 = 10	2 x 10 = 20	3 x 10 = 30
1 x 11 = 11	2 x 11 = 22	3 x 11 = 33
1 x 12 = 12	2 x 12 = 24	3 x 12 = 36

4 TIMES TABLE	5 TIMES TABLE	6 TIMES TABLE
4 x 1 = 4	5 x 1 = 5	6 x 1 = 6
4 x 2 = 8	5 x 2 = 10	6 x 2 = 12
4 x 3 = 12	5 x 3 = 15	6 x 3 = 18
4 x 4 = 16	5 x 4 = 20	6 x 4 = 24
4 x 5 = 20	5 x 5 = 25	6 x 5 = 30
4 x 6 = 24	5 x 6 = 30	6 x 6 = 36
4 x 7 = 28	5 x 7 = 35	6 x 7 = 42
4 x 8 = 32	5 x 8 = 40	6 x 8 = 48
4 x 9 = 36	5 x 9 = 45	6 x 9 = 54
4 x 10 = 40	5 x 10 = 50	6 x 10 = 60
4 x 11 = 44	5 x 11 = 55	6 x 11 = 66
4 x 12 = 48	5 x 12 = 60	6 x 12 = 72

Children start by learning the 2, 5 and 10 times tables at around ages six to seven, so start playing with those first.

7 TIMES TABLE

7 x 1 = 7
7 x 2 = 14
7 x 3 = 21
7 x 4 = 28
7 x 5 = 35
7 x 6 = 42
7 x 7 = 49
7 x 8 = 56
7 x 9 = 63
7 x 10 = 70
7 x 11 = 77
7 x 12 = 84

8 TIMES TABLE

8 x 1 = 8
8 x 2 = 16
8 x 3 = 24
8 x 4 = 32
8 x 5 = 40
8 x 6 = 48
8 x 7 = 56
8 x 8 = 64
8 x 9 = 72
8 x 10 = 80
8 x 11 = 88
8 x 12 = 96

9 TIMES TABLE

9 x 1 = 9
9 x 2 = 18
9 x 3 = 27
9 x 4 = 36
9 x 5 = 45
9 x 6 = 54
9 x 7 = 63
9 x 8 = 72
9 x 9 = 81
9 x 10 = 90
9 x 11 = 99
9 x 12 = 108

10 TIMES TABLE

10 x 1 = 10
10 x 2 = 20
10 x 3 = 30
10 x 4 = 40
10 x 5 = 50
10 x 6 = 60
10 x 7 = 70
10 x 8 = 80
10 x 9 = 90
10 x 10 = 100
10 x 11 = 110
10 x 12 = 120

11 TIMES TABLE

11 x 1 = 11
11 x 2 = 22
11 x 3 = 33
11 x 4 = 44
11 x 5 = 55
11 x 6 = 66
11 x 7 = 77
11 x 8 = 88
11 x 9 = 99
11 x 10 = 110
11 x 11 = 121
11 x 12 = 132

12 TIMES TABLE

12 x 1 = 12
12 x 2 = 24
12 x 3 = 36
12 x 4 = 48
12 x 5 = 60
12 x 6 = 72
12 x 7 = 84
12 x 8 = 96
12 x 9 = 108
12 x 10 = 120
12 x 11 = 132
12 x 12 = 144

VIDEO GAME MATHS

When I first thought of this game, I used a little Super Mario figure to encourage Ewan to join in. We'd recently been to a friend's house; they had a Nintendo Switch™ and Ewan would probably do ANY chore I gave him just to have half an hour of playing Mario Kart with his friends. So, as always, whenever my kids show an interest in something I try to turn it into a game that wedges something useful into it (but you can use any figure in this game based on your own kiddo's interests).

GRAB:

- paper
- pen
- scissors
- 10 cups
- 2 coins
- small toy figure

TO SET UP . . .

1. Write five multiplication number sentences on the sheet of paper and cut them out. On separate bits of paper, write the correct answer to each number sentence, as well as a wrong answer.
2. Line up the cups in five pairs. Put a correct answer and a wrong answer under each pair and the corresponding number sentence on top of the two cups, creating a little bridge.
3. Place a coin under two of the wrong answers.
4. Put the toy figure by the first bridge.

TO PLAY . . .

1. Explain to your child that the figure needs to jump across all the bridges to reach the end. In order to clear a bridge, your child must find the correct answer.
2. Move the figure to approach the first bridge. Ask your child to read the multiplication number sentence and tell you the answer they are looking for.
3. They then choose a cup and lift it up. If it is the correct answer, their little figure can jump across the bridge and go to the next bridge.
4. If it's the incorrect answer, they have to take their figure back to the start, shut their eyes and you replace the bridge and answer, swapping the answers under the cups if you like.

5. If they get an incorrect answer but find a coin, that is a LIFE. They can choose to either use their life immediately and continue to the next bridge or go back to the beginning and save their life for the next attempt and use it if they get the wrong answer again.

6. Keep playing until they reach the final bridge. Don't be afraid to add sound effects like 'Wheeeee!' just as they do in computer games! If your kiddo is enjoying it, tell them they've reached the next level, then write and cut out some more multiplications for them.

VARIATION

■ You can adapt this game for any kind of number sentence, if you want your kiddo to practise addition, subtraction or division.

This game can also be played with a ping-pong ball and three cups.

THE THREE TARGETS

I don't know about you but it was an exciting day in our house when I realized I could own more than ONE laundry basket. I could have as many as I like . . . I'm an adult, after all! So I bought myself three. Which means there is always at least one of them knocking around to play with (usually with some odd socks at the bottom) and they're the perfect things to throw balls into!

GRAB:

- 3 baskets or large receptacles like a laundry bin
- a soft ball (use balled-up socks if you don't have one) or a bouncy ball
- pen
- paper
- pencil

TO SET UP . . .

1. Next to each basket, write the times table that your child is working on. For example, if you're practising the 2, 5 and 10 times tables, write '2' on the paper in front of one basket, '5' on another and '10' on the third.
2. On another sheet of paper draw three columns with the multiplier numbers to match at the top (see photo opposite). For example: '2x', '5x' and '10x'.
3. On the same sheet draw twelve horizontal lines to create twelve rows, and write the numbers 1 to 12 down the left-hand side.

TO PLAY . . .

1. Explain to your child that they have to throw the ball at the baskets and see which one it lands in. Whichever basket the ball goes in, starting with the first row of the paper grid, they have to times the row number (the multiple) by the basket multiplier. They then write the answer in the correct column in the grid.
2. Each time the ball goes in a basket, fill in the next row of the matching column. So, if the ball lands in the '2' basket three times the '2x' column should read 2, 4, 6 (along rows 1–3, respectively).
3. Keep going until they've filled every row and column (if they can) or they can have a certain number of throws. Then see which multiplier number won with the most multiples.

GRIDBLOCK

Using a grid like the one on page 227 to support your child when introducing times tables can be helpful. For some children, the idea of working out the answers can seem hugely daunting. In a similar way to how I've often suggested we play with words to familiarize our little ones with them before they have to learn how to spell them, I also recommend playing games where the answer is readily available at the beginning. This can help to build confidence, which is always worth doing.

GRAB:

- chalk
- bean bags (if you don't have bean bags, fill a sandwich bag with some uncooked rice and seal it)
- pen, paper and scissors – or multiplication number sentences on flash cards
- a container

TO SET UP . . .

1. On the floor, draw a grid for the times table you're working on, in the same style as the one shown on page 227.
2. Write and cut out multiplication number sentences (for example, 3 x 2 = and 6 x 2 =) to match the grid (or grab your flash cards – see page 7), and pop them in the container.

TO PLAY . . .

1. Take it in turns to draw a number sentence out of the container. Together, work out the answer using the grid.
2. As soon as you've got the answer, both throw your bean bags at the number in the grid on the floor. The first one to get it to land on the correct answer gets to keep the number sentence.
3. The winner is the one with the most number sentences at the end!
4. Try to (gently!) block each other as you shoot for the target if you like. Get competitive and run around the grid or try to hit each other's bean bag mid-air!

You could also set this up as a slide with a longer cardboard tube propped up and the child sliding the correct tens and ones balls to you.

TENS AND ONES SHOOTER

As I noted at the beginning of this chapter, whereas when I was at school we would say 'tens and units', these days in schools teachers refer instead to 'tens and ones'. And they also use the word 'digit' rather than 'number' when it comes to tens and ones. So in this game we can practise that. And by 'we' I'm referring to us, the grown-ups, because I can confirm that the kids take great delight in correcting us 'oldies' when we accidentally ask 'How many units is it?'!

GRAB:

- cardboard tube or plastic cup with the bottom cut off so it becomes a tube
- a balloon
- tape
- 2 different colours of paper or tissue paper
- a pack of cards
- 2 containers

TO SET UP . . .

1. Make a shooter: tie a knot in the balloon and cut the top off; attach it to the tube as shown, with tape to secure it. (See photo opposite.)
2. Scrunch your paper into small balls.
3. On one container write **TENS** (10s) and on the other write **ONES** (1s).
4. Pop all the balls of one colour into the **TENS** container and the other colour into the **ONES** container.
5. Remove the jacks, kings, queens and jokers from your pack of cards. An ace equals one.

TO PLAY . . .

1. Turn over two cards and show them to your child. Explain that the first card is the tens digit and the second card is for the ones digit. Can they tell you what number the two cards make? So a 3 and a 6 would make 36.
2. They then have to fire the correct amount of tens and ones balls at you to make 36. Encourage them by asking questions like 'How many tens are there in thirty? And how many ones are in the 6?'
3. If you like, you can try to catch the balls or you could set up a target.

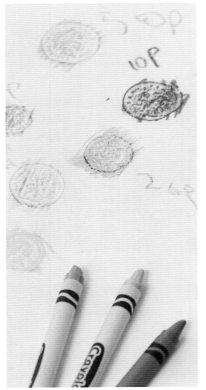

SHOW THEM THE MONEY!

Introducing money to children can be tricky. As adults we are so familiar with coins and notes and their value that it's quite hard to imagine looking at them and finding them all completely strange. I can remember as a child wondering why my parents said we couldn't afford things when they could just go to a cash machine and get more money out. It didn't occur to me that it wasn't a never-ending supply. Understanding the economy seems quite a lot to teach a kid. So let's break it down, penny by penny, and have fun.

1. COIN RUBBING

An old classic. Grab a soft pencil and some paper. Pop the coins under the paper (I stick them to the surface underneath with Blu-Tack so they don't wiggle around) and rub away. We sometimes also draw the number of dots to match the value of the coin next to each rubbing, if the kids are in the right mood for it.

2. SORT IT OUT

Get a load of coins (we collect spare change in an old sweetie jar!) and tip them on to the floor or a table. Sort them into piles of different amounts. You can also build towers, look at what's on each coin, and try to find ones that match.

3. TOY SHOP

Grab a few toys and write a price on a bit of paper for each of them. Get a purse or wallet and put some real money in it. Your kiddos can buy the toys from you using the correct coins.

4. TUCK SHOP

When it is time for a snack, quickly grab some paper and write a price on each of the snack items on offer. Give your child some money and see which item they wish to buy. Can they afford it with what they have? How much change will they get? How many ways could they pay for it out of the coins they have?

5. COIN CUPCAKES

Get some paper cupcake cases. Write different random amounts on each case. Give your child a handful of coins and see if they can make up the correct amounts by putting the coins into each case. So, for example, for a case that has '16p' written on it, they might pop in a 10p, a 2p and four 1p coins.

OLD FIVE-MINUTE GAMES REIMAGINED

Naturally we still often play some of the games from my first book, *Give Me Five*. In fact, these are the games I most often revert to when I'm tired or in need of something fast and guilt-free, because I must confess to using my book like many of you do, by grabbing it and flicking to our old favourites. However, don't worry if you haven't got a copy, because I've updated a few of them so you can play them with school-age kiddos and keep up the maths learning at the same time . . .

1. TOY TOMBOLA

For this game, line up twenty small toys (you can use your tat box for this – for more on what that is, go to page 8) and then write a number on each ticket for your kids to 'win' each toy. When Ewan and Florence were little, the tickets were just for the numbers 1 to 20 and they would pick one out and then count along the line to see which toy they had 'won'. Now, though, instead of writing the number on the tickets, I write a number sentence. So if the number sentence says **3 + 1 =** then your child counts along the line of toys (up to number 4) to win their toy. I mix up number sentences for addition, subtraction, multiplication and division, so it's just one big maths game.

2. PASTA POSTING

This was an idea that I used regularly when my kids were toddlers to buy myself five minutes' peace. I'd get a small box, pierce holes in it and then give them some dried pasta to post through the holes. Even as they got older, they still loved this game, so I started using it for numeracy instead. When they were just learning to recognize numbers, I'd write a number next to a hole to post that many pasta pieces through. But as they got older I started writing number sentences and times tables on the box too. They used the dried pasta to help them work out the answer and posted it through the holes. If I'm in the mood, I sometimes draw monster faces with the amount required written in speech bubbles. I then tell them to get busy feeding the monsters, while I crack on with feeding my own monsters, and stick some tea in the oven.

3. SPIDER'S WEB

This is a firm favourite with me and for many of those who follow my social media channels, who have sent me messages to say how much they love it, and I hope you'll enjoy this game too. The beauty of the spider's web is its simplicity. In the early days I would just write the numbers from 1 to 10 on a piece of paper and the challenge would be for my little ones to join them up consecutively with a line. Nowadays I use this for times tables practice and write down the answers to a times table all around the page, and then it's up to the kids to join them up in the correct order. Don't forget that you can always do this on the floor in chalk, or with a ball of string and numbers scattered around a room.

4. WASHING LINE

Another game for times tables that is super easy. Write the answers for a particular times table on sticky notes or small bits of paper. Grab some masking tape and tape a strip between two chairs or similar with the sticky bit facing you. Then ask your child to pop the numbers on to the tape in the right order. So, if they were doing the 5 times table, they'd start with 5 and then they'd need to try to find the 10, then the 15, and so on. This is a great way to introduce times tables for the first time, as you can count together and stick up the notes.

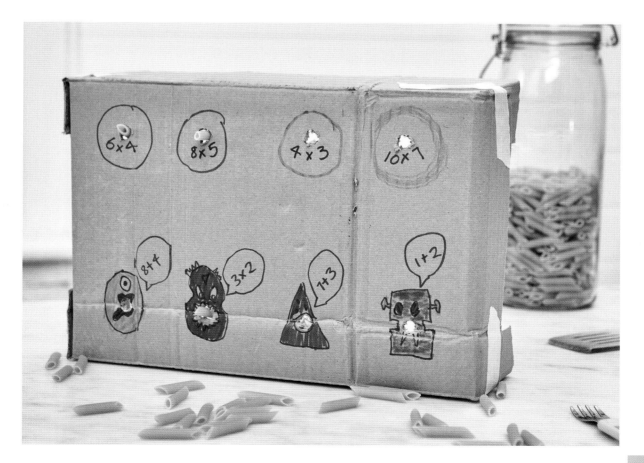

NUMBERS IN A NUTSHELL

I hope that, especially if you are a bit number-phobic like I am, this chapter has given you some ideas of ways to make maths seem a little less daunting for both you and your kids. It's very common as a parent of a school child to unknowingly pass any anxieties or difficulties we had at school on to our own little ones. Our schooling has a significant impact on us as we grow up and so it's only natural that visions of our experiences will come flooding back into our mind as we relive it all through the tiny humans we are nurturing.

But we must also remember that they are their own people. Their slate is clean. Their experience will be their own, and our job here is not to hide our emotions but to acknowledge them and talk about them in a useful way. I often tell Ewan that maths wasn't Mummy's favourite subject – not so that he will think I didn't enjoy it and will shy away from it but because I want him to see that, even though it seems through his six-year-old lens that Mummy and Daddy are oracles on almost everything, actually we are only human too. We have flaws and insecurities and we can discuss them and talk with our little ones about ways we overcame, or are still overcoming, them.

So, maths for me is a perfect reminder that we all have limitations and there will come a time when Florence and Ewan, who is a little numbers whizz already, will leapfrog my understanding entirely and will probably start teaching me. I encourage them all I can. They know that Mummy doesn't find maths easy, but they also know that I still loved school and playing, and when we play maths games together it makes me happy. We can't always be good at everything – but the fun is in discovering what we're able to do, and we might even find that we can do a lot more than we ever imagined.

LIFE SKILLS

FIVE-MINUTE LIFE SKILLS

FIVE-MINUTE LIFE SKILLS

There are a lot of things for our little ones to learn in the first few years of being on Planet Earth, aren't there? And the things only get more varied as they skip up the year groups at school, where they cover all manner of topics. One of the things I have enjoyed most about having children who attend school is them teaching me something new. Their little sponge-like brains absorb information at a miraculous rate and they will occasionally surprise me with a wonderful regurgitated fact. It's sheer joy! But there's also a lot more to their learning than reading, writing and maths as we well know. So how do we pass on some of these additional life skills to our kiddos?

Well, I've saved this last chapter for short and sweet ideas to play around with the kind of things they will cover at school but that will also be helpful for their everyday lives. These ideas are good for those rainy days during school holidays or when you feel like your brains are all melting after a day in front of the TV. They teach life skills that we all need under our belts at some point or another, and that are often covered by teachers in classrooms rather briefly as they try to cram as much as they can into their coverage of an already overstuffed curriculum!

In order to gather the kind of topics that would be useful, I spoke to some wonderful primary school teachers. I asked them, 'What do you wish your pupils had knowledge of that could easily be done at home?' And their answers included things like telling the time and tying shoelaces – which kiddos can certainly learn through play, as I'll show you over the next few pages.

So I hope these five-minute ideas for building skills can provide a bit of fun alongside something useful. On days where everything seems to drag, I turn to these activities to help pass the hours and erase my guilt if I've ignored the kids for a bit when I've had to crack on with something else that required my attention. They came in especially useful during the lockdown periods of the 2020 pandemic when noses were turned up at worksheets sent from school!

After years of being **FIVE MINUTE MUM**, I can you tell this: it actually doesn't really matter WHAT you're teaching your little one at home. It's the spending time together doing something that's the important bit. If you're a fan of angling and they know the name of every bit of fishing tackle going, you're still doing something hugely valuable. I love gardening, so my children are skilled at planting seeds and are starting to know the names of a few plants. It doesn't matter what it is that you love doing. Introduce it, relish it and don't ever see it as a waste of time just because it isn't on the curriculum. Remember that old saying? Kids spell *love* like this: **T-I-M-E**. Cheesy, but absolutely true.

DAYS OF THE WEEK AND MONTHS OF THE YEAR

The whole concept of time can seem baffling to a child who lives in the moment. I've made countdown calendars on scraps of paper for my kids before, where we cross off days or count the sleeps until exciting events, to stop the relentless 'Is it my birthday yet?' questions. Here are some other ideas to get to grips with how we register time passing.

1. SING A DAYS OF THE WEEK SONG

There are a few different ones online but our favourite is the one that goes to the tune of *The Addams Family*, which my kids sing at school. It goes:

> There's Sunday and there's Monday,
>
> There's Tuesday and there's Wednesday
>
> There's Thursday and there's Friday
>
> And then there's Saturday.
>
> Days of the week *CLAP CLAP* Days of the week *CLAP CLAP*
>
> Days of the week, Days of the week, Days of the week. *CLAP CLAP*

2. CALENDAR

When it gets to around February or March, you often will see the current year's calendar on sale in shops, sometimes for as cheap as 50p. If you grab one, it's a handy resource for kids. Or save your own from last year if you have one. Your little ones can flip through the months and write their birthdays and other family members' birthdays too.

3. ANAGRAMS

Grab some magnetic letters and a baking tray. Make the word **day** by sticking the letters to the tray, then gather the following letters: one each of **a**, **d**, **f**, **h**, **i**, **m**, **n**, **o**, **r**, **s**, **t**, **u**, **w** and two of **e**. Scatter them around the edges of the tray. Challenge your child to work out which letters they need to add to day to spell out what day it is today, then do yesterday and tomorrow, putting the letters back around the edges each time.

4. SOUND IT OUT

Teach your kids to pronounce the days as they are spelled, to help them remember the spellings. For example, **WED-NES-day**. Say '**wed**' as in wedding and '**nes**' as in Loch Ness monster – perhaps embellish with a story about how Wednesday is the day that the Loch Ness Monster got wed! You can also do this for **MON-day**. Make the *o* sound the same as in the word *cot* so it reminds them it isn't *u* making the /uh/ sound and helps them to spell it.

5. MAKE A DAILY CHART

Get a piece of cardboard and make a chart as shown in the picture below. Cover it with sellotape or sticky-back plastic, then update it with a whiteboard pen, filling out the day spaces and changing the month name on a monthly basis. Rub it out with a cloth to start each new day.

When Ewan started school, I found some 'days of the week' socks. They were plain black but with the days of the week written in different colours along the sole, so he loved selecting the correct socks for the day. Mind you, it did add quite a bit of pressure to get them washed in time!

Talk to them regularly about how there are sixty seconds in a minute, sixty minutes in an hour and twenty-four hours in a day. When my little ones ask 'How long until . . . ?' I often switch up my answer, and say 'In sixty seconds' instead of 'In a minute' so they're reminded that it's one and the same.

TELLING THE TIME

What's the Time, Mr Wolf? Do you remember this game? My kids absolutely love it and it's a great way to introduce them to the 'o'clock' part of time. You could play this game and, instead of saying the time, hold up a home-made clock, so they have to figure out the steps from the time. (A quick internet search will give you the rules if you don't know them.) Or you could try some of these wee tricks to while away the hours . . .

1. CLOCK DECK

You can play this with a deck of playing cards. Lay them out like a clock with: the ace where 1 would be; a jack for 11; a queen for 12; and a king in the middle (as shown on the opposite page). Let your child sort the remaining cards into their correct places. Perhaps time them to see how fast they can sort the whole pack. Or you could give the kiddos a deck of cards each and see who is the first to sort all their cards into the clock places. Teach them to play Clock Patience (check online for instructions to play).

2. TIME BALLOONS

On a quiet day at home, write five activities you would like to do on bits of paper. It could be bake biscuits, ride bikes, play a board game . . . anything you like. Then put each bit of paper into an empty balloon. Fill each balloon with air and tie it, then write the time you'd like to do the activity on the balloon. When that time swings around on the clock, get your kids to read the time and find the right balloon. They can then pop the balloon and find out what activity is next. Mind you, this is only fun if your kiddo isn't scared of loud noises! (If they don't like loud noises, like my Flo, you could use little boxes instead of balloons.)

3. CLOCK PAIRS

Cut out twenty-four equal bits of thin card by folding two pieces of A4 card in half three times. On twelve cards draw clock faces with different times on each of them. On the other twelve cards write the same times in sentences or as a digital twenty-four-hour time (for example, quarter past four or 16:15). Now mix them up and lay them face down and play a game of pairs, taking it in turns to turn over two cards and seeing if the times shown on them match.

4. MAKE A CLOCK

You could do this out of LEGO®, or blocks and lolly sticks, or using some card or a paper plate with a split-pin in the middle. Any way you like, just spend five minutes making one.

5. BE THE CLOCK

Draw a clock on the floor using chalk. You shout out some times and your kids use their bodies to be the hands. Their bum is on the centre, with their legs as the big hand and arms as the small hand.

COMPASS GAMES

You can complicate these games as much as you wish based on your child's ability. Start with the main compass points – north, south, east and west – but as they get older you can progress to include north-west and south-east, and eventually move up to the heady heights of north-north-west and so on. Although, I have to say, this level of specificity isn't something I have ever used in real life . . . !

For both these games you need to make a **SIMPLE SPINNER**. Here's how:

GRAB:

- cardboard
- pencil
- pen
- scissors

TO MAKE . . .

1. Cut the cardboard into a square and write **N** on one edge of the square, then **E** on the next edge, **S** on the next and **W** on the remaining one. (See the photo below.)
2. Using the scissors, make a hole in the middle of the cardboard square, then push the pencil through it.
3. Now you can spin the pencil on its point and the spinner will randomly land on **N**, **S**, **E** or **W**.
4. If you wish to make a spinner that includes the mid-points, like north-east and south-west, cut out an octagon instead of a square.

SPINNER BLOW FOOTBALL

This is best played on a smooth floor surface if that's available.

GRAB:

- your spinner
- paper, pen and scissors
- tape (masking tape is best as it doesn't tend to mark surfaces)
- a lightweight ball like a ping-pong ball (or a screwed-up bit of newspaper) for each player
- a straw for each player

TO SET UP . . .

1. In the room where you are playing, choose north, south, east and west points. They don't have to be geographically accurate (unless you want them to be!); just do it so they match the layout of a compass.
2. At each point, create a paper tunnel by cutting the paper into a strip and taping it to the floor at either end so it forms an arch as shown in the photo below.
3. Write **N**, **S**, **E** or **W** on the tunnel depending on which compass point it is.

TO PLAY . . .

1. Spin the spinner.
2. Whatever direction it lands on, each player has to blow their ball through the correct tunnel as quickly as they can, starting in the centre of the play area.
3. First one through the tunnel wins a point. Then spin again.
4. Play as long as you like – we usually have to continue until the kids beat me!

You can also play this game with toy cars instead of balls and straws. You have to push your car from the centre of the room and try to get it through the tunnel.

Don't forget these silly sentences to remember the order of the compass points: Naughty Elephants Squirt Water, or Never Eat Soggy Waffles. Can your kids come up with their own sentences?

TREASURE ISLAND

GRAB:

- your spinner
- a large bit of cardboard
- a pen
- a counter (small figures will do) for each player
- a dice

TO SET UP . . .

1. On the cardboard, draw a grid of twelve by twelve squares.
2. Write **N**, **S**, **E** or **W** on the correct sides.
3. Next to **N** roughly draw a treasure chest; next to **E** draw a shark; next to **W** draw a crocodile; and at **S** draw the sea with a boat in.
4. Draw a star in one of the squares in the middle of the grid.

TO PLAY . . .

1. The youngest player starts. They place their counter on the star and spin the spinner. Whichever direction the spinner lands on is the direction their counter will move in.
2. Then they roll the dice to see how many spaces they will move in that direction.
3. After they have moved, the next player puts their counter on the star and has their turn.
4. Continue this, with each player spinning the spinner and rolling the dice to move around the grid.
5. If a player falls off the grid on **E** or **W**, they are eaten by the creatures and have to return to the star. If they fall off at the bottom (south), they go to the ship and miss a turn before returning to the star.
6. Keep playing until someone gets the treasure at **N** by reaching the top of the board.

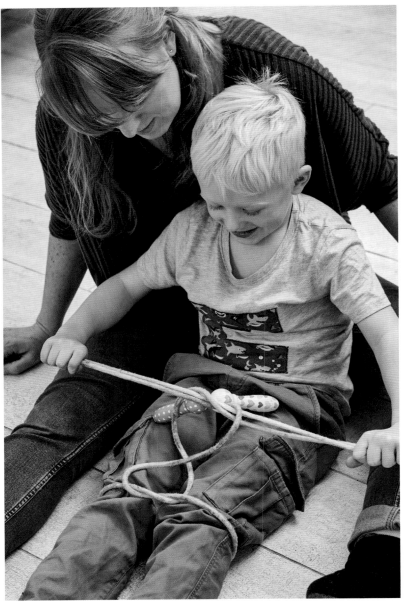

If you've got *Give Me Five*, you can also try these dressing games: Coat Race, Sock Chalk Game and Dress the Chair. And I've got more ideas on my website: fiveminutemum.com

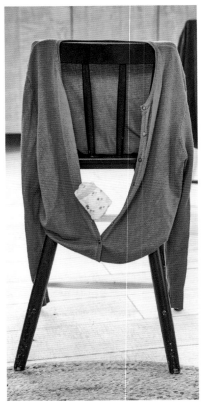

'PUT YOUR SHOES ON!'

Have you shouted this before? Multiple times, until you are blue in the face? Please say yes, because I need to know it isn't just in our house! Learning to put on shoes and socks, and just generally get dressed, is obviously a useful life skill. Some kids have an innate self-motivation to want to do this and take the path of fierce independence. Others, however, need vast amounts of encouragement to not become a permanent nudist. My son falls into the latter camp, so here are some of the games we have played.

1. GIANT'S LACES

If you have a skipping rope or a long piece of rope, tie your child's legs together with a bow, so they can see the actions of tying laces in giant form, from the correct perspective. Let them tie your legs up too.

2. TISSUE–BOX SHOES

The novelty of something different is often a good way to capture a child's imagination. Use two empty tissue boxes, poke holes in them and tie some laces to mock up a pair of shoes. Two different-coloured laces or strings can also be massively helpful for them to see which bit of lace goes where for the knot.

3. CARDIGAN GAME

Get two cardigans with the same number of buttons on them if you can. (If not, just do up some buttons so the number of undone buttons on each of them matches.) Hang the cardigans over the backs of two chairs as shown, with the bottom button fastened so it creates a sort of hoop. Now, each grab some balled-up socks, sit leg length away from the chair and try to throw your socks through the hoop you've created, which is the neck of the cardigan. If you score, you do up a button on your cardigan. First to have all their buttons done up wins.

4. DRESSING TOMBOLA

Grab a few bits of paper and either draw or write down items of clothing that your child has at home. Fold them up and pop them in a container and let your kiddo pick out one item at a time so they have to get dressed in a funny order.

5. THREAD

Any kind of threading activity is brilliantly helpful for little hands learning how to do up zips and buttons. You could thread beads on to pipe cleaners, pop hooped cereal or crisps on to dried spaghetti or sticks standing up in play dough, or thread string through the holes in a colander. Anything you like that gets those fingers gripping and threading.

MAKING SNOW
1. Get an empty squeezy drinks bottle.
2. Pop in about five tablespoons of liquid soap or shampoo, and a tiny splash of water.
3. Shake it like crazy for as long as you can!
4. Squeeze your 'snow' out anywhere you like to create a snow scene.
5. Add food colouring for rainbow snow.

ROYGBIV is the colour order of a rainbow. Can you make up a silly sentence with your kids to remember the order?

Rodents Often Yell Good Bye In Vans?

WEATHER AND SEASONS

Living in England means that our weather is gloriously unpredictable, and seasons come and go like a slow-moving kaleidoscope. Weather features highly in topics we talk about, so it's important to involve the kids in that too. When I was little, whenever we went on holiday my dad would always put the song 'Weather with You' by Crowded House on the car stereo and we'd all sing along! It's a soundtrack I recommend for any of these games!

1. MAKE A RAINBOW

On a sunny day, get a glass of water and put it near a window where the sun is shining through. You might have to shift it around a bit, but if you get the right angle you can create a rainbow in your house. Stick a bit of plain paper to wherever the rainbow appears and let your child capture it by colouring in over its magical colours.

2. RAINFALL PREDICTING

Save some empty plastic containers from the recycling bin, and do some rainfall predicting by each drawing a line of where you think the rain level will get to. You could vary the days or even hours if you like and see who is closest with their prediction. Measure the rainfall afterwards with a ruler too.

3. FAN RACES

Create a simple fan by folding paper into a concertina, going one way, then the other. Then get a bit of lightweight paper like tissue paper or toilet paper, draw a leaf on it and cut it out. On a floor, create a start and finish point, and use your fans to waft the leaves with the wind you create from your fans. The first leaf over the finish line wins.

4. WEATHER SCENES

Use a shallow tray and set up a scene using play figures. They can be dolls or plastic figures or anything you like, but something waterproof is best. If it is autumn outside, scrunch up some dried brown leaves and pop them on the tray for the figures to crunch through. If it's spring, perhaps add some grass and small wild flowers, and if it's winter, make snow foam – find out how to make snow in the box opposite!

5. WHAT SEASON AM I?

When you're made to wait for a few minutes if you're out and about with the kids or in the car, say 'What season am I?' and then give them clues. For example: 'The trees are very green, there are no clouds in the sky, butterflies are all around . . . I AM . . . ?'

MEMORY GAMES

Memory games are so important at this age. A lot of what we are asking our children to do is memorize masses of information. They are like little computers that we are constantly plugging in to update. Sometimes their memories get clogged up and overloaded. Sometimes they falter, like all of us. So the best way to keep them running smoothly is to play some games that exercise those memory muscles.

1. GENERATION GAME

Gather together ten to fifteen random items or toys in a line. Tell your child to walk along the line, slowly naming all the items; then they have to turn their back to the items. Set a timer for one minute and see how many they can remember. Then let them put you to the test and see who wins by remembering the most!

2. I WENT TO THE ZOO

This is a classic memory game you can play in the car or anywhere you like to keep kids entertained. Just start a story with the sentence 'I went to the zoo and I saw . . .' and then say an animal. Then it's the next person's turn; they say the same sentence 'I went to the zoo and I saw . . .' and they say the first person's animal and then add their own. You keep going until there is a long list of animals to remember.

3. WHO WAS WHAT?

Grab flash cards with the numbers 1 to 6 on, six soft toys and a dice. Give each toy a random flash card, look to see what number it is, then place it face down next to the toy. Roll the dice. Which toy had that number? Can you remember?

4. FIVE-POINT STORY

Tell them a story where five things happen. See if they can tell the story back to you, remembering all five things. For example: 'Yesterday me and Florence got dressed in tutus, then we went to the shops for some oranges, afterwards we went on the swings at the park, then we ate some cupcakes, and finally we went home to watch a movie. What a nice day. Can you tell me what we did on my imaginary day?' Then let them tell you an imaginary day and you try to recall it.

5. ANY PAIRS

Any kind of matching pairs game is great. You can play with tricky words, spellings words, number sentences, number bonds, times tables, letters, phonics sounds. Anything you like. Make two sets of flash cards (see page 7) and off you go.

This sounds obvious but, if there is an international sporting event on, try to show some of it to your kids on the TV. This is a great way to show them different people from different countries, and discuss where they come from, their national anthems, traditional dress and history.

WHERE ARE WE?

Explaining that there is a big wide world out there, and that we are located in one tiny speck on it, is quite a tricky thing to get across to children. Especially when they sleep for two hours on a journey and say 'That was quick!' when you arrive. Explaining to them how land is divided up isn't the easiest. We've played around with these ideas at home to help my kids' understanding for when they cover geography topics in school.

1. MAKE FLAG BUNTING

I cut out lots of rectangles of paper, and we chose flags from different countries to colour in ourselves. We then taped all the flags to a long bit of string and hung them up. As we coloured, we chatted about each country.

2. SPEND THE DAY THERE

If you have a quiet day at home planned in the holidays, then make it 'FRENCH DAY' or any country you like. Make or try some food from that country, watch some videos about it online, read any books you have about it, do a mini quiz for family or friends. Just make the whole day all about the country.

3. CAPITAL HUNT

Write the names of ten countries on bits of paper, including the four countries of the UK if you live there, and pop in a bag or container. On ten other bits of paper, write the capital cities of those countries. Hide the capitals around a room. Take it in turns to pull a country out, then set a timer and see how fast you can find its capital. Then someone else has a turn. See who can get the record for the fastest match-up, or (if only one child is playing) see which country capital you find the quickest.

4. PIN THE CITY ON THE COUNTRY

In a large space, draw a rough map of the UK on the floor in chalk or with masking tape. Label the countries and roughly where the capital cities are. Blindfold your child and then say a city. See if they can walk to it. They tell you when they think they've found it and take off their blindfold to see how close they were. Then you can have a turn. Can anyone land exactly on the correct city?

5. MESSY MASSES

Use some cooled, cooked spaghetti to make the outline of countries. Let your child stick the spaghetti on to paper to match a land outline (use a book, atlas or internet images as reference) or you could do this with play dough and make the land mass. You could even make some flags out of cocktail sticks and paper if you like, to stick into each country you've created.

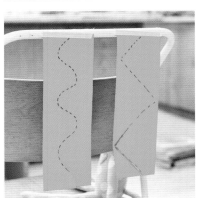

If you have got a left-hander, make sure you get special left-handed scissors for them. You can buy safety scissors for children online or in shops.

SCISSOR SKILLS

If you hold a pair of scissors and then try to explain to someone how they actually work, you suddenly realize what a specific skill it is. It's something that comes mostly with practice, because a description doesn't really help matters. Some children can grasp scissor use with a few goes and get the hang of it, but for others it can take a bit of time. Remember to only use safety scissors with kiddos. As always, be led by your child and try to make it as fun as possible with some quick and easy play. Oh, and obviously it goes without saying: these are games that need grown-up eyes on them at all times!

1. TOILET-ROLL HAIR CUTS
Save a few empty toilet rolls and draw some faces on the side. Then use safety scissors to cut into them to create hair. Let your child cut their hair or redesign it. For little ones who find card tough to cut through, create the tubes with paper and sticky tape.

2. TABLE TAPE
Get a long piece of paper. Draw different line styles on it lengthways, then tape one end to a table or a chair, as shown in the photo opposite. Let your child stand and cut from the end upwards to the table, following the lines.

3. DOUGH CUT
Get some play dough and roll it into sausage shapes. Leave it out on a tray with some scissors for your child to investigate. Cutting up play dough is actually incredibly satisfying! Include some sticks on the tray to build with the cut-up pieces too, if you like.

4. PAPER DOLLS
This is a lovely activity that is probably centuries old. We have the book *The Paper Dolls* by Julia Donaldson (which always makes me sob!) so we often read this, then make our own. See ours on the opposite page.

5. MAKE PERFUME
Go outside together and collect some petals, flowers and leaves in a pot. Half fill a bowl of water and let your child cut up the foliage and flowers into the water to make their own 'perfume'.

TOPICS

During the course of school, your child will probably be introduced to different classroom topics. I can vividly recall becoming mildly obsessed with Ancient Egypt after a particularly brilliant teacher captured my imagination with some really fun activities around pyramids and pharaohs. Children can cover ANY number of vast and interesting topics over their school days, but when they do it's sometimes nice to join in at home if it's something that's especially taken their fancy. Here are some of the ways you can support topic learning.

1. TIMELINES

During history topics, children are often asked to make timelines and put events into the correct order. There is a skill to doing this, which we can practise at home. Choose any story book, and on bits of paper write down or rough draw five things that happen in the story and cut them out. Now read the book with your child. Afterwards, show them the pieces of paper and see if they can put them into the correct order, along a line from left to right, to match the events in the story.

2. CATEGORIZING

This is another fantastic skill that will come in hugely handy. If your little one is doing a topic such as animals, they might need to know different categories of animal. These could be anything: herbivores, carnivores, omnivores; predators and prey; feathers, scales or fur; even mammals, reptiles, insects, and so on. You can play games at home that prepare your kids for this. Gather a big handful of random toys. How many ways can you categorize them? By colour? By size? By type? Just spending five minutes sorting is playful organization that will benefit them (and also you, because the toys get sorted out!). A pack of playing cards is also an easy way to sort. By suit? By colour? By number? Let your child choose.

3. FACT–FINDING

Play Two Truths, One Lie. Do you know this game? So, if your child is perhaps doing a space topic at school, you could explain: 'I am going to tell you three things. Tell me which one is the lie. Mars is a planet. Neil Armstrong was the first man on the moon. Astronauts only eat sausages.' This simple game you can play anywhere, any time, is a great way to help them fact-find.

4. PREDICTION GAMES

Science-based topics often include predicting, experimenting and then discussing the outcome. We can do this at home with simple games like Sink or Float: get a bucket of water and ask your child to find ten items (that can safely go in water), write down the names of the items and predictions (will they sink or float?) and what actually happens after they've been plopped in the bucket. We have also done this with cars going down a ramp. Which will go furthest? Guess, then push them down and measure the distance they travelled. Get your kids to write down the outcome, then discuss why one car goes further than another. All great stuff!

5. GET CREATIVE

This is definitely not my speciality but, if your child is really captured by a topic at school, use it to your full advantage. Pop online and you'll find craft activities for any topic you could imagine. Get out the paper, paint and glue, and let your kiddos go wild creating. Just remember to tape newspaper to all the surfaces first to make for a quick clean-up!

Some of my favourite topics include mini beasts (teaching them about insects), people who help us (discussing people like police officers, fire fighters and postal workers), dinosaurs, space, light and dark (discussing night-time and daytime, nocturnal animals, electricity and so on) – but ask your child's teacher what they are covering this year at a parents' evening if you want to know!

DISCUSSING RACISM AND PREJUDICE

These are huge topics that obviously cannot be covered with a few quick games. However, it is something I want to highlight because these are definitely matters that we as parents or caregivers need to pay attention to. Because the time to talk about this is NOW. At any age, there is an appropriate way to discuss racism and prejudice with your children. It's useful for us to explain it is something that sadly exists in our world, and to talk about how we can behave as human beings to ensure 'being kind' isn't just something we say or hashtag, but something we actually practise.

I have written an extensive blog post filled with resources on anti-racism on my website. If you have five minutes, then pop over and give it a read, because I truly feel this subject should be heard about from people who have lived experiences. I have listed child-friendly links to helpful videos and educational resources for parents and children alike.

However, here are five things you can do to facilitate conversations with your kids on this biggest of topics. Because what I truly believe, as with everything in this book, is that little and often is best. Constant small reminders and discussions will build a foundation that hopefully means our children feel they can talk to us about anything. Communication and understanding are the tools we can equip them with, to help build a world where racism and prejudice are eradicated from our future. Yes, our schools definitely have a part to play too, but it starts, I believe, at home.

If you spend any time with small children, then you have direct access to the future of our world. So let's use that to influence them in a way that changes it for the better. We won't get it right 100% of the time. But that's OK. When do we ever, as humans, get it all right? When we realize we've made a mistake, let's hold our hands up and make changes. We can't ever be perfect, but let's never stop learning.

1. CHECK YOUR RESOURCES.

Look at the toys and books in your home. Do they reflect the diverse world we live in, or do they just represent one type of person? If it's the latter, next time you decide to buy your child a book or a toy, perhaps consider buying something different that reflects people who live differently or look different to you. Libraries are always useful if you cannot afford to buy something new, and TV shows can often provide new perspectives too. Seek them out.

2. TALK TO YOUR CHILDREN ABOUT DIFFERENCES.

We might feel that when children are oblivious to the differences in humans that their innocence is to be protected. But the reality is that at some point they will become aware and, if we haven't discussed it with them, they might reach their own conclusions from things they've overheard from others. Take control now. Explain differences and talk about them regularly, highlighting how what we see from the outside is just one very small part of a complex individual, who has thoughts, hopes, dreams and feelings exactly the same as them. Books are perfect for this, and there is a list of our favourites on my website **fiveminutemum.com**.

3. EDUCATE YOURSELF.

Feeling a bit out of your depth discussing it? That's OK. Take some time to educate yourself as a parent first. I've listed some useful resources on my website, including social media accounts, which I found intercepted my mindless scrolling with useful information. Being consciously aware of some of the problems is a useful first step. I will be the first to admit that in the past I haven't been as consciously focused on this topic as I should have been. Admitting this and taking action to change it is something we can all do.

4. TALK TO SCHOOL.

Speak to teachers or the school your child attends about how they discuss racism and prejudice with the children. Use their guidance if you're a bit unsure. Ask them how they present and cover the topics, and, if you feel there is something that needs to be challenged, open up a discussion through the correct channels.

5. BE A MODEL.

Try this – ask your child to touch their elbow, but, as you say it, touch your shoulder. They will probably touch their shoulder too, even if you loudly repeat 'Touch your elbow' while still touching your shoulder! As with everything, children learn more from seeing what we **DO** than listening to what we **SAY**. If they see you treating people fairly and kindly, they will mimic and copy this. If you hear or see someone act in a racist or prejudiced manner and you dismiss it, they will learn to do the same. Model the behaviour you wish to see in them. If you see someone treated unfairly, act in any way you can to demonstrate this is not something you are willing to accept.

EMOTIONS AND MENTAL HEALTH

Now you might be under the impression, because of the vast number of activities in this book, that I am the kind of parent who has perfect children, who sit nicely doing wholesome activities all day long. You might believe that I am in an apron in my kitchen, floating around serenely as my children craft and play beside me.

If you have that impression, then I hate to burst your bubble, but that definitely is not me. I'm the 'reality' version of that social media image. The one with her frazzled hair tied up on top of her head, the tired look on her face, and the weary voice that says 'Are you sure?' – knowing full well that they really are NOT sure and that the consequences will be catastrophic.

Like every parent or person who spends large amounts of time with small children, I am often breaking up squabbles, dealing with tantrums and trying to handle big emotions from my children, and wondering if my response is good enough.

Occasionally when we are playing the games you are reading about in this book, one of my children will 'kick off'. Sometimes it's because they aren't winning. Sometimes it's because they aren't in the right mood or, although they thought they wanted to play, they now don't. Sometimes it's because it isn't the game they wanted, even though they specifically asked for it. There really are no rules for when tensions run high and emotions become fraught.

Now I know for certain that this isn't just my kids, and it isn't just your kids. It is just KIDS. Children are small humans and, like you and me, they feel different at different times. Think of your mood today . . . Are you relaxed? Angry? Fed up? OK? You could have any number of feelings right now. Your kids are the same, but they don't yet have the experience, vocabulary or emotional intelligence to identify their different emotions and know how to handle them. They are at sea. Sometimes the waters get stormy and they shout for help.

So, what are my tips for this? Oh, crikey. I wish I could supply all the answers but I can't. I'm not a behavioural expert, nor can I claim to even have got this right with my own kids. I am learning every single day. But school can help and here's why. In schools, as part of the curriculum, teachers spend time focusing on PSHE which stands for Personal, Social, Health and Economic Education. In these lessons, children will cover lots of things from healthy eating choices to relationships and mental wellbeing.

Teachers will take time in the classroom to talk through and teach the children strategies to encourage them to understand their emotions and what to do if they are struggling. We can, of course, support this at home in lots of different ways. Here are just five things I have found useful for when feelings become heightened:

1. CARVE OUT FIVE MINUTES.

Spend at least five minutes of your day asking your child how they feel. Put away any distractions for both you and them, and simply talk. Weave it into your routine if you can. Making chats about feelings a regular thing can be incredibly useful to help increase their vocabulary around emotions.

2. CHANGE LOCATIONS.

Often when one of my children is getting particularly cross, I take them to a new location. So I might pick them up and walk around my garden, calmly describing what I see, or move them to a different room and find a toy or something to distract them. This worked particularly well with Florence when she had just started school and I found she was often tired and emotional.

3. STAY CALM.

Trial and error has taught me that if I get cross in my responses we get nowhere. If I stay calm, my little ones often find safety in my calmness. It isn't easy but it's worth the effort of ten deep breaths before responding to a tantrum.

4. GIVE THEM SPACE AND TIME.

Sometimes when Ewan has become massively frustrated when we're playing, or perhaps is struggling to deal with the fact he is losing the game, he will get upset. If this happens, I always let him have some space and time before speaking to him. I've often found that, if I leave him to calm down, he will return to play again later and then we can discuss what happened in a more useful way.

5. 'ALL FEELINGS ARE OK'.

Ewan said this to me when he was five. I think he had heard it at school in a PSHE session, but it really resonated with me. What a lovely idea. All feelings are OK. How we feel is how we feel. It's OK to feel. We now regularly repeat this to each other.

If you feel your child is struggling with their emotions, perhaps they are particularly anxious or worried or becoming angry and cross quickly, then please speak to their teacher. They might well have some strategies they can share from the PSHE programme they are following that you could continue with at home. Most schools have staff who are specifically trained to work with children whose behaviour has become challenging due to their emotions, so don't ever feel like you cannot open up a discussion with them to talk through your child's needs.

Books are an invaluable resource when it comes to emotions. There are so many books out there designed to support small children and understand their emotions. Libraries are, of course, a fantastic way to discover new ones, and don't forget you can always ask librarians to order ones you might specifically want.

ROLE PLAY

And, finally, one of the best techniques I have discovered for emotional support in children? Play. It always comes back to play. Playtime isn't just for occupying them. Playing IS learning when it comes to children, and that includes learning about themselves, emotions, social constructs, conflict resolution and mental health. One of the best tools for this is DOLLS. Any kind of doll. But dolls that represent humans in play have been scientifically proved to activate the part of our brains that we use during social interactions, even when children play alone. So, having access to a doll is massively important. The reason all Early Years settings have role-play corners is so that children can play out social scenarios in a safe space.

But does it have to be a doll? Of course not. Time spent playing is never wasted when it comes to children. So bookmark a page of this book, pop out their favourite board game, or just join in with whatever they are already playing. I think what amazes me most about those five minutes spent playing is that my mental health benefits as much as the kids'.

WE ALL NEED PLAYTIME.

PLAYING IS LEARNING

Let's get something straight as we finish this book off. I'm not playing these games to MAKE my kids learn. I don't play them so my children come top of the class in everything academic they do. I am not trying to trick them into knowing their times tables or phonics through games.

WE ARE PLAYING FOR FUN.

For them, and me. When we play games that have a challenging element in them, I find that it adds interest for me too. I always love to see how they will respond and if they will take to it. When we get that magic combination of shrieks of joy alongside absorption of knowledge, it can make you feel, for that split second, like you are getting everything right.

But this isn't a given. Frustrations and tantrums are always only one wrong move away and, if at any point we aren't enjoying the game, we stop playing. It isn't work. It's **PLAY**. The learning is a by-product.

Here's the thing. **ANY** play is learning. Not just games that I have written about here that have numbers and letters and words and bits from the school curriculum in them. Playing with dolls is learning. Driving a remote-control car is learning. Playing with blocks is learning. Riding their bikes around a cul-de-sac is learning. Building dens is learning. Playing with play dough and sticking random bits of cardboard and tissue paper together is learning.

IT ALL COUNTS.

In order to encourage our children to grow up as developed, rounded individuals, ready to achieve their full potential, we want to provide them with access to lots of opportunities. School will consistently offer new things to try, but there are limits to what a school can provide. Your child might get to bake once a term but they might also love to cook and want to do more. Or your kiddo might really enjoy rock climbing, but there's no way to practise that in the playground. Or they might love chess, but there isn't a school chess club.

This is where play comes in and why it's so important. Through play, we can watch our children and observe what they gain the most pleasure from in the world. If we can nurture that and encourage it, by converting their joy of making cupcakes into allowing them to take over the kitchen regularly, or enrolling them in a rock-climbing club so they can scale walls to their heart's content, we are setting them up for a life of living playfully.

Play brings us all **JOY**. Even adults. Think of what you enjoy most, and I expect there might be an element of play in it. And if you allow yourself to completely give in to play occasionally with your child, by building your own plastic brick masterpiece or riding your bike as fast as you can down a hill alongside them, then I suspect you'll find a place where contentment resides. It's what often makes us think that kids have really got it all figured out a lot better than us adults do!

So, yes, the games are educational – of course they are. But their purpose is fun. It's joy. It's laughter and silliness. It's mindfulness and living in the present moment. And if you feel your stern 'we must do this' inner voice creeping in during these five-minute games, take a moment to pause. Put it away. Get out Snakes and Ladders, suggest hide-and-seek, dig out the blocks, dolls or a play kitchen. There is JUST as much to be gained from doing those things as there is a game with times tables. And don't for a second think that I don't stick on the telly when we've all had enough, because I absolutely do!

Playing is learning. And if you do nothing else with your five minutes except join in with your child's play, then know that that is plenty. Your kiddos have decades of adulting ahead of them. But, for this short period of time, their priority is **FUN**. So, for five minutes a day, make it yours too. I promise you won't regret it.

ACKNOWLEDGEMENTS

Enormous gratitude firstly to all the teachers and teaching assistants out there. For taking on our wee nippers and dedicating your life to sharing knowledge in an interesting and impactful way – never ever underestimate the importance of what you do. There are a few special teachers I would like to single out:

MISS COONEY – when I first started writing this book, Ewan was in Samantha's Year One class. He adored her and so, when I wanted some guidance on what to include in this book, I asked her, and she kindly devoted time to pulling together a document that I referred to constantly throughout writing. Thank you.

MRS SOUDERS – a great friend and a constant source of information for all things teaching, especially maths-related. Gemma, without our kitchen-brew chats and you replying to my confused WhatsApp messages this book would've made a lot less sense!

MISS BOWEN – it's always lovely when your sister-in-law-to-be is someone you really like and get on with. It is even better if they are a fantastic Early Years teacher, with tons of knowledge who can help you out with all kinds of random queries! Meghan, I will pay you back in babysitting any time.

MRS MOORE – your phonics knowledge powered me through the longest chapter of this book. Your support and guidance are always hugely appreciated by me and everyone else who follows you online (@miniwritersclub). Anna, thanks so much for devoting precious time to help me out even when it was in short supply.

Also, I would like to thank some teachers who had an impact on my life. I highly doubt they will ever see this but if you taught at Halsford Park Primary School in the 90s I owe you a huge debt of gratitude. Thanks to Mr Nye, Mrs Mac, Ms Morgan, Mr Lovelady and countless others at Imberhorne School. As the years have gone on, I've appreciated what you taught me more and more.

To Mr Merrell and the staff at Oldfield Brow Primary School in Altrincham. The start you have given my children to their school years couldn't have been bettered. The smiles on their faces after a day at school is all I need to see to know what a superb job you're all doing. Thank you.

Thanks also go to those at Penguin Random House for their incredible support during the wildly exciting book ride I've been on this year. Special thanks to Wendy Shakespeare whose organizational and editing skills have provided calm and support throughout the entire process of pulling this book together. Thanks also to Ruth Knowles for your guidance and editorial notes, which make me laugh out loud.

A big **WE DID IT** and thank you to the design and photography team who made this book look so beautiful despite lockdowns, restrictions and everything in between. On the photo shoot were Nikki Dupin, Lol Johnson, Ben Hughes, Pippa Shaw and Charlie Goodge who worked incredibly hard, in masks and within tight limits across all three days and beyond to make this book happen. It would be incredibly dull without their efforts, so cheers to you all!

Gratitude as always to Lauren Gardner for being the best literary agent ever. Your phone calls always cheer me up! My thanks and love also go to the team who are constantly behind me no matter what – my mum and dad, Willie and Jeanette, and my friends and family who constantly offer words of support and encouragement.

And finally to my little gang. My husband, Kenny, who puts up with everything behind the scenes that goes into Five Minute Mum – me stressing about writing or manically chopping up cardboard and rifling through baskets to find something specific for a game, thereby creating chaos in my wake. I know I must drive you bonkers at times, but thanks for always being there and letting me do it anyway.

To Florence and Ewan. You are at the heart of everything in this book. Your willingness to always try out Mummy's silly games is what keeps me going. You are my sunshine, always, and I cannot thank you enough for allowing me to keep doing what I do. It's been fun, hasn't it?

Lastly, thank **YOU**. Yes, **YOU**. The person reading this book. There are occasionally times where I think I will just go back to being Mummy, playing games at home and telling no one, because it was so much easier. But every time I do, I get a message from a reader, often accompanied by a picture, and I cannot express enough just how much joy it brings me. I am so grateful to every single one of you who plays the games in my books with the children in your lives. I wish you all happy playing!

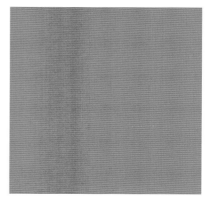

INDEX